WILD
COSTA
RICA

WILD COSTA RICA

The Wildlife & Landscapes of Costa Rica

Adrian Hepworth

First published in 2008 by New Holland Publishers (UK) Ltd
London • Cape Town • Sydney • Auckland
www.newhollandpublishers.com

Garfield House, 86–88 Edgware Road, London W2 2EA, UK
80 McKenzie Street, Cape Town 8001, South Africa
Unit 1, 66 Gibbes Street, Chatswood, New South Wales,
Australia 2067
218 Lake Road, Northcote, Auckland, New Zealand

10 9 8 7 6 5 4 3 2 1

ISBN 978 1 84773 113 5

Senior Editor: Krystyna Mayer
Design: Alan Marshall
Cartography: Stephen Dew
Production: Melanie Dowland
Commissioning Editor: Simon Papps
Editorial Direction: Rosemary Wilkinson

COVER AND PRELIMINARY PAGES
Front Cover: Keel-billed Toucan (*Ramphastos sulfuratus*).
Spine: Poison Dart Frog (*Dendrobates pumilio*).
Back Cover: The Del Toro waterfall.
Page 1: Cloud forest orchid (*Cochleanthes discolor*).
Page 2: Red-eyed Tree Frog (*Agalychnis callidryas*) on a spiral
ginger flower (*Costus woodsonii*).
Page 3: The Talamanca mountain range seen from the summit
of Mount Chirripó.
Page 5: Purple-throated Mountaingem (*Lampornis calolaema*)
at orchid (*Elleanthus glaucophyllus*).
Page 6, from top to bottom: Leaf cutter ants (*Atta* sp.);
Tree Frog (*Hyla rufitela*); Arenal Volcano at sunrise;
Yellow-naped Parrot (*Amazona auropalliata*).
Page 7: Monteverde Cloud Forest Preserve.

Reproduction by Pica Digital (Pte) Ltd, Singapore
Printed and bound in Singapore by Tien Wah Press

CONTENTS

INTRODUCTION

The wild and rugged landscapes of Costa Rica represent a journey into a very different world from the environment that many of us are used to.

Visitors can trek through dense rainforests where Jaguars roam, watch a volcano throw out rivers of molten lava or lie on beaches that remain as wild as they were when Christopher Columbus first anchored his ships off the Caribbean coast in 1502. The more adventurous may scuba dive with schools of Hammerhead Sharks or scramble up the summit of Costa Rica's highest peak to marvel at views of both the Pacific and the Atlantic Oceans.

Throughout these wild and diverse terrains lives a plethora of wildlife that is for many the most fascinating attraction of all. Costa Rica has a higher density of recorded animal and plant species than any other country in the world. To put this into context, Costa Rica has eleven times as many bird and mammal species per 1,000 sq km as Colombia does. Compared with Indonesia, another wildlife-rich country, it has twenty times as many bird and plant species and fifteen times as many mammal species per 1,000 sq km.

Scientists have recorded 240 species of mammal, 860 species of bird (which represent 8 per cent of the world's total), 221 species of reptile and 174 species of amphibian in Costa Rica. In addition, more than 10,000 species of plant have been

OPPOSITE: *The Los Crestones rock formation sits on the treeless, sub-alpine* paramo *above the cloud forests of Chirripó National Park.*

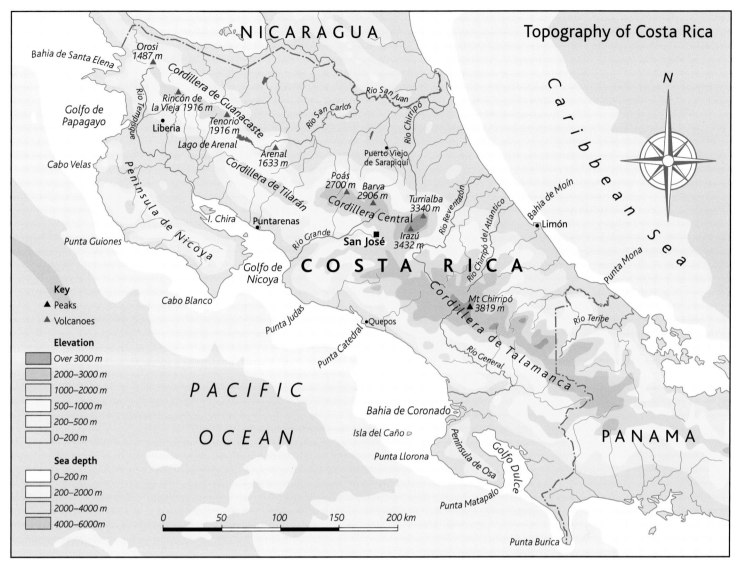

LEFT: *The sun sets beyond the calm waters of Manuel Antonio National Park.*

identified with another 2,000 believed to remain undiscovered, and a staggering 370,000 species of invertebrate are estimated to live in Costa Rica, of which 350,000 are insects. In all, between 3 and 4 per cent of all the world's animal and plant species can be found in Costa Rica. This figure becomes all the more astounding when we consider that, with a land area of just 51,100 sq km, Costa Rica represents only 0.03 per cent of the world's total land surface area; it is less than half the size of England, not much larger than Switzerland or Belgium and more than eight times smaller than the US state of California.

Of the vast array of species that inhabit Costa Rica a significant number are endemic, which means they are not found anywhere else on the planet. The Costa Rican National Institute of Biodiversity (INBio) lists 6 species of mammal, 7 species of bird, 36 species of amphibian, 36 species of reptile and 1,100 species of plant in Costa Rica as endemic. The enormously rich biodiversity in Costa Rica is a consequence of two

main factors: firstly, the enormously varied topography and wide variety of natural habitats that exist within its borders, and secondly, the fact that over millions of years it has been populated by a wealth of flora and fauna from two different continents.

In 1947 an American botanist, Leslie Holdridge, designed an elaborate system that classified areas of Central America into different life zones according to their mean annual temperature, rainfall, humidity, latitude and elevation. Based on this system, there are twelve different life zones in Costa Rica, each with its own particular natural vegetation and variety of fauna. Sub-alpine, treeless *paramo* surrounds the peaks of Costa Rica's highest mountains at elevations of 3,500 m and more. The highest of these, Mount Chirripó, stands at 3,819 m above sea level and experiences temperatures that drop to below freezing point. These mountains form part of a series of *cordilleras* that run north-west to south-east down the length of the country. Both their Pacific and Atlantic slopes are cloaked with cloud forests and rainforests, many of which receive 4–5 m of rainfall per year. In some areas of the Atlantic lowlands, for example Tortuguero National Park, this figure can reach an extraordinary

ABOVE: *The Northern Tamandua (*Tamandua mexicana*) is one of many mammal species that migrated from South America to Central America when the land masses joined, roughly 3 million years ago.* OPPOSITE: *Tourists in rainforest in Manuel Antonio National Park.*

many more species were able to move freely from one continent to the other, including land mammals that had previously been unable to cross the water; monkeys, anteaters, porcupines, agoutis, sloths and armadillos came from the south, and cats, tapirs, deer and foxes arrived from the north. These migrations are largely responsible for the enormous biodiversity that exists in Costa Rica today.

Today, a large proportion of Costa Rica's animal and plant species inhabits protected areas of wilderness that cover 20 per cent of the country's land territory. It is a system of government- and private-owned parks, reserves and refuges that has been developed over the last 50 years and fuels what is now Costa Rica's largest industry – tourism. These protected areas attract more than a million visitors every year, and it is this interest in tropical beaches, steaming jungles, active volcanoes and exotic wildlife – and the money it generates – that is central to the survival of these wild places.

There is a strong symbiotic relationship in Costa Rica between the natural environment and the companies and local communities that practise responsible ecotourism or directly benefit from it. The many people that this work involves fully understand how introducing tourists to nature can provide a comfortable standard of living for themselves and their families. As a result, they protect their source of income.

Some communities and hotels keep turtle-nesting beaches clean of rubbish and natural debris and provide tours for visiting tourists, which they guide in small, unobtrusive groups. Numerous landowners have set aside areas of forest for ecotourism rather than clearing them for agriculture, and many one-time poachers have now become nature guides on these same properties. Of course, there are some hotels, travel operators and guides that do harm the environment during the course of their activities, despite what their logos suggest, and it is up to tourists to plan their trip with this in mind.

In Costa Rica, both governmental and non-governmental organizations play a very important and influential role in the protection of wild areas. In recent years a number of different bodies have purchased significant areas of land with which to increase the size of national parks, biological reserves and wildlife refuges and to link them to one another via biological corridors. If this work can continue successfully, the wild areas of Costa Rica and the plants and animals that live within them will be enjoyed for many generations to come.

7 m. On the opposite side of the country, in the lowlands of Guanacaste, tropical dry forests thrive in temperatures that regularly pass 30°C and experience a four-month drought at the beginning of every year that causes most trees to lose their leaves. Annual rainfall in parts of this region is less than 1 m.

The creation of present-day Costa Rica began roughly 50 million years ago during the early Paleogene period. The convergence of the Earth's Cocos and Caribbean tectonic plates below the ocean caused countless volcanic eruptions that gradually began to construct a series of islands between the land masses that are now known as North and South America. Some plant and animal species from the two continents flew or floated across the ocean to these islands and began to populate them, although the number was relatively small. Eventually, these islands became a continuous strip of land and, roughly three million years ago, the land that now includes Costa Rica became the bridge that connected the northern and southern continents for the first time. As a result,

CHAPTER 1
HABITATS & FLORA

Some of the greatest competitions on Earth take place in the tropical rainforests of Costa Rica. Within 1 sq km of virgin forest, hundreds of different species of tree contend for the light they require to stay alive. In their shadows, a host of shrubs and saplings vies for the few rays of sun that filter through to the ground far below. And throughout these forests, many tens of thousands of animal species from the big cats to tiny poison dart frogs employ myriad ingenious tactics in their battle to reach reproductive age and pass on their genes to the rainforests' next generation of animals.

LEFT: *Rainforest blankets the steep, mountainous slopes of Juan Castro Blanco National Park.*

RAINFORESTS

The tropical rainforests of Costa Rica can be generally described as those areas of evergreen forest below the cloud layer that receive at least 2 m of rainfall per year and do not experience prolonged dry periods. They grow in a patchwork of areas of various sizes in the lowlands and on both slopes of the mountainous cordilleras that bisect the country. Rainforests in Costa Rica generally grow to a maximum elevation of around 1,000 m, where the transition to cloud forest vegetation occurs. The sticky air inside the rainforest is typically warm and loaded with humidity.

GEOGRAPHY AND CLIMATE

Rainforest on the Caribbean or Atlantic slope grows within a triangular area between the slopes of Orosi Volcano in the north-west, Barra del Colorado Wildlife Refuge in the north-east and Gandoca-Manzanillo Wildlife Refuge at the southern extremity of Costa Rica's Caribbean coastline. The largest areas of protected rainforest in this region are Braulio Carrillo National Park, Barra del Colorado Wildlife Refuge, Tortuguero National Park and La Amistad International Park, which follows the Talamanca Cordillera south into Panama.

The Caribbean slope is the wettest area, with some locations receiving up to 7 m of rainfall annually. It also has more regular rainfall during the year than the Pacific slope. Partly as a consequence of this, biodiversity in Costa Rica seems to reach its peak at elevations of around 500 m on this slope.

OPPOSITE: *Dense rainforest vegetation surrounds a stream in Braulio Carrillo National Park.*
BELOW: *The Violet Sabrewing (*Campylopterus hemileucurus*) often feeds on heliconia flowers in highland rainforest.*

On the Pacific slope, the most northerly area of rainforest grows in Carara National Park, where the River Tárcoles meanders its final few kilometres towards the ocean. Only tropical dry forest grows north of this region because the land experiences a dry season of several months with little or no rain – conditions that rainforest plant species cannot tolerate.

Fragments of rainforest exist on the coast south of Carara, including in Manuel Antonio National Park, which is one of the few remaining sanctuaries of the endangered Squirrel Monkey (*Saimiri oerstedii*). The largest area of rainforest on the Pacific slope is in and around the Osa Peninsula, which contains the world-famous Corcovado National Park. Inland, there are areas of protected rainforest on the slopes of the Talamanca Cordillera in La Amistad International Park and Chirripó National Park.

THE FOREST

The astonishing diversity and magnificent proportions of Costa Rica's rainforests leave visitors with an unforgettable sense of awe. Due to the multitude of different plant types and the tangle of vegetation that they create, from every turn of a trail the forest looks quite different.

Some of the oldest rainforest trees in Costa Rica are higher than most of the buildings in San José. The Kapok Tree (*Ceiba pentandra*) and the Tonka Bean Tree (*Dipteryx panamensis*) are two examples of such giants. The most mature trees tower up to 60 m above the ground, with their lowest branches emerging at a height of 30 or 40 m. The Kapok Tree grows in rainforests country-wide, and the Tonka Bean Tree is a native of the northern Caribbean lowlands. These trees stand taller than most other rainforest trees and as a result are known as emergents. The unobstructed, 360-degree views from the tops of these trees make them ideal perches from which large birds of prey such as eagles can scan large areas of forest for their prey. The Tonka Bean Tree is vital to the continued survival of the magnificent Great Green Macaw (*Ara ambigua*) in Costa Rica as it provides that species' favourite nesting site – the macaws lay their eggs in the hollows of the tree's dry branches.

The leaves of the emergent trees are smaller than those of shorter trees because they are much more exposed to the wind. Smaller leaves create less resistance and therefore the strain at the base of the tree is kept to a minimum. Despite this adaptation, the largest emergents still require tree trunks that are 2–3 m thick at their base to help keep the tree upright.

Below the emergent trees, the canopy layer of Costa Rican rainforests usually forms between 20 and 40 m above the ground, depending on the age of the trees. Here, trees of many different species extend their branches in fierce competition with their neighbours for space and the light it provides. This

LEFT: *Rainforest in Corcovado National Park overlooks the Pacific Ocean.*

level of a rainforest has the richest biodiversity. The maze of branches provides walkways for monkeys and many other mammals, the height of the canopy keeps birds' nests out of the reach of most predators, and lizards, snakes, frogs and invertebrates find an abundance of food among the dense foliage.

Many of the rainforest animals in Costa Rica that feed and sleep in the canopy also spend time closer to the ground; the White-faced Capuchin (*Cebus capucinus*) regularly forages for fruits and insects on the forest floor or will drink from a puddle of water in the mud. It often travels between the canopy and the ground via long vines such as the appropriately named Monkey Ladder (*Bauhinia guianensis*), which has an undulating stem that provides convenient footholds and handholds for climbing animals. Other canopy-dwelling animals that are often found close to the ground include vultures, which descend to the forest floor to feed on carrion, and many frogs, which migrate down from the treetops to mate and care for their eggs during the rainy season.

Many other species that live in the canopy rarely or never venture close to the forest floor. The chameleon-like Canopy Lizard (*Polychrus gutturosus*) and the nocturnal Annulated Tree Boa (*Corallus annulatus*) usually don't leave the upper reaches of the forest in their entire lifetimes.

Below the canopy of a tropical rainforest is an area known as the understorey. The amount of vegetation that grows here is mainly dictated by the age of the larger trees. In primary rainforest, where the trees have not been felled and then regrown, the oldest specimens form a continuous canopy that allows only a small percentage of the sun's light to reach the forest floor. As a consequence, few plants grow in the spaces between tree trunks.

Those plants that do exist must be very shade-tolerant and able to survive in the low light conditions. Young canopy trees that manage to germinate are suppressed in their juvenile state, sometimes for years, until one of the large trees dies or is blown over by strong winds. The light that streams through the gap left by the fallen tree triggers a race between saplings to fill the space with their own leaves.

Secondary rainforest, which has been cleared in recent times and then left to regrow, has younger, smaller trees than primary forest, and so forms a less dense canopy that is closer to the ground. This allows much more light to penetrate down to the forest floor and therefore many more shrubs and small trees grow in the understorey.

The understorey vegetation of both primary and secondary rainforests in Costa Rica produces a vast array of exquisite flowers. The largest flower in Costa Rica, and indeed Central America, is the Dutchman's Pipe (*Aristolochia grandiflora*),

RIGHT: *Enormous buttress roots provide stability to many tall rainforest trees, which grow to heights of up to 60 m.*

ABOVE: *The Dutchman's Pipe (*Aristolochia grandiflora*) is Costa Rica's largest flower. Fully grown ones measure up to 40 cm wide.*
ABOVE, RIGHT: Heliconia latispatha *is one of about 30 heliconia species that add splashes of colour to Costa Rica's forests.*
OPPOSITE: *Rivers and streams help to remove some of the huge quantity of rainwater that falls on the rainforest.*

which is a rare species but grows in rainforests throughout the country. Its 40 cm-wide purple and white flower produces an odour very similar to that of rotting meat. Flies are fooled by both the sight and smell of the newly opened flower, and follow its strong scent into a convoluted tube that opens in the centre of the flower. Their escape from this tube is blocked by small hairs inside the entrance and, during their frantic attempts to leave, they collect the flower's pollen on their bodies and wings. About twenty-four hours after opening – enough time to ensure the flies inside have picked up its pollen – the hairs inside the flower collapse, allowing the flies to escape. When the flies enter a new flower, they pollinate it with pollen carried from the old flower, completely unaware of their role as the plant's pollinator.

The understorey vegetation close to the ground grows in the coolest and most humid area of the rainforest. This area is the habitat of amphibians such as the poison dart frogs, which rely on the high levels of moisture for their survival. Plants here typically have large leaves that have pointed ends, called drip tips, which allow rainwater to quickly drain away. This helps to prevent the growth of bacteria and fungi on the surface of the leaves. The dark and damp forest floor provides the perfect microclimate for these organisms, which play an essential role in the decomposition of dead animals and plants and the recycling of their nutrients. An estimated 13 per cent of all living species in Costa Rica are fungi.

Countless small streams, canals and rivers flow through the rainforests of Costa Rica. They carry with them most of the rainfall that neither evaporated nor was not taken up by plants and transpired back into the air. Incredibly, even though these waterways transport a large volume of water from rainforest soil, it is only about a third of the amount that either evaporates or is transpired. For this reason, when an area of rainforest is cut down, the land is easily flooded by heavy rains.

Heliconias

About thirty species of heliconia grow in Costa Rican rainforests, and their vividly coloured bracts are impossible to miss in the understorey of the rainforest. The actual flowers are the small, curved structures that grow out of each bract. The shapes of these flowers match the bills of the hummingbirds that pollinate them, and the bright red pigment in many heliconia bracts is the colour that most attracts these birds. The sharply curved bill of the White-tipped Sicklebill (*Eutoxeres aquila*) allows the bird to perch on heliconias such as *Heliconia reticulata* and feed on the upright flowers. The Rufous-tailed Hummingbird and the Violet Sabrewing (*Campylopterus hemileucurus*) feed on less curved heliconia flowers such as *Heliconia latispatha* because they have much straighter bills.

Numerous other animals seek food, refuge and even camouflage from heliconias. Many birds, such as motmots, trogons and tanagers, feed on the fruits that heliconias produce. White Tent Bats (*Ectophylla alba*) rest under the long leaves of heliconia plants during the day. They gnaw the leaf on either side of its midrib so that the two sides droop down, thus creating a three-sided refuge that hides them from predators. The bright

OPPOSITE: *The long nose of the White-nosed Coati (*Nasua narica*) gives it a keen sense of smell for locating animal prey and fruits.*
BELOW: *White Tent Bats (*Ectophylla alba*) huddle under a heliconia leaf during the day, sheltered from predators, sunlight and rainfall.*

yellow morph of the Eyelash Viper (*Bothriechis schlegelii*) sometimes curls around the bracts of a heliconia in order to ambush hummingbirds that come to feed or lizards and frogs that pass by.

THE FAUNA

A walk through a tropical rainforest in Costa Rica will reveal the enormous variety of plant species that combines to make the forest what it is. A sharp-eyed walker can also begin to pick out the animals that live there. Often the best way to see wildlife, however, is to simply sit down and have a rest. Within a relatively short time a significant number of animals will have walked, jumped or flown past your chosen spot. The majority of those seen will be invertebrates and birds, though lizards, frogs and mammals are also often observed during a quiet rest. Even a coiled snake or one on the move may be spotted. While taking one such break I was lucky enough to watch a Puma (*Puma concolor*) creeping through the undergrowth just 15 m away from me.

Up to half of the planet's animal species are believed to live in tropical rainforests around the globe. The huge biodiversity that is so evident in rainforests in Costa Rica strongly supports this theory. Mammals of many different families and of all sizes

live in the rainforests of Costa Rica; they range from tiny mice that can disappear under a leaf on the forest floor to the country's largest land animal, the 250 kg Baird's Tapir (*Tapirus bairdii*). They also inhabit every level of the rainforest, from the ground up to the canopy.

At the top of the food chain are the largest cats of the New Tropics, the Puma (*Puma concolor*) and the Jaguar (*Panthera onca*), which hunt their prey on the forest floor and occasion-

ally venture up a tree to make a meal of a sloth or monkey. Four other species of cat also live in Costa Rica's rainforests.

Several other sizeable mammals frequent the forest floor. Herds of White-lipped Peccaries (*Tayassu pecari*) roam through Corcovado National Park, which is almost their last remaining refuge. Their smaller and more common relative, the Collared Peccary (*Tayassu tajacu*), also lives in rainforest but is much more widespread. Red Brocket Deer (*Mazama americana*),

ABOVE: *The Squirrel Monkey (*Saimiri Oerstedii*) is the rarest of four Costa Rican monkeys, surviving in isolated parts of the Pacific coast.*

Tayras (*Eira barbara*), White-nosed Coatis (*Nasua narica*) and Northern Tamanduas (*Tamandua mexicana*) are also present.

The Giant Anteater (*Myrmecophaga tridactyla*) is on the brink of extinction in Costa Rica, though recent evidence suggests it still inhabits rainforest on the Osa Peninsula. Another endangered mammal, the Squirrel Monkey (*Saimiri Oerstedii*), lives exclusively in the rainforest of the central and south Pacific lowlands, while Costa Rica's other three species of monkey, the White-faced Capuchin, the Mantled Howler Monkey (*Alouatta palliata*) and the Spider Monkey (*Ateles geoffroyi*) live in rainforests around the country.

Another tree-dweller is the Silky Anteater (*Cyclopes didactylus*), which feeds on arboreal ant colonies. Meanwhile the similarly placid Hoffman's Two-toed Sloth

(*Choloepus hoffmanni*) and Brown-throated Three-toed Sloth (*Bradypus variegatus*) hang from branches or lianas, feeding on their favourite leaves.

Dozens of species of bat roost and feed in the rainforest. One common species on both slopes is the Proboscis Bat (*Rhynchonycteris naso*), groups of which spend the daylight hours sitting arranged in a vertical line on a tree trunk. Presumably this formation makes the bats less conspicuous to predators. Their brown and grey fur looks very similar to tree bark and completes their camouflage superbly.

Hundreds of species of bird brighten the rainforest with their intense colours and lively behaviour. The enormous-beaked Chestnut-mandibled Toucan (*Ramphastos swainsonii*) and the Keel-billed Toucan (*Ramphastos sulfuratus*) are popular symbols of Costa Rican rainforests, which they inhabit on both Pacific and Caribbean slopes. Along the central and southern Pacific coast, life-long mated pairs of Scarlet Macaws

ABOVE: *The Chestnut-mandibled Toucan (*Ramphastos swainsonii*) breeds in rainforests on both coasts of Costa Rica.*

(*Ara macao*) squawk loudly as they fly together over the trees, and in the northern lowlands there is the chance of glimpsing the Great Green Macaw.

Among the dozens of birds of prey that live in the rainforests of Costa Rica there are five species of eagle, including the Crested Eagle (*Morphnus guianensis*) and Ornate Hawk Eagle (*Spizaetus ornatus*). The largest eagle of the Americas, the Harpy Eagle (*Harpia harpyja*), may still survive in the country despite the lack of confirmed sightings in recent years. Another majestic bird of prey, the King Vulture (*Sarcoramphus papa*) perches in the tallest trees to survey the surrounding rainforest for signs of carrion. The Montezuma Oropendola (*Psarocolius montezuma*) is another bird of the canopy, which builds 1 m-long nests that swing in the breeze. The camouflaged plumage of the Great Potoo (*Nyctibius grandis*), a crow-sized bird related to the nightjars that also lives in the canopy, keeps it hidden from predators during the day. Over 30 species of humming-

bird reside at least seasonally in Costa Rica's rainforests, and among the many other attractive birds that dart through the vegetation are trogons, motmots, tanagers and manakins.

Reptiles and amphibians abound in the hot and humid environment that a rainforest offers them. In Costa Rica more than 150 species live in this type of forest. Snakes such as the Boa Constrictor (*Boa constrictor*) and the Fer-de-Lance (*Bothrops asper*) ambush small mammals on the forest floor, while the Eyelash Viper and Palm Pit Viper (*Bothriechis lateralis*) capture lizards and frogs in shrubs and trees close to the ground. Brightly coloured poison dart frogs hop across the leaf litter and high above, in the canopy, the Red-eyed Tree Frog (*Agalychnis callidryas*) waits for the first heavy rains of the wet season, when it descends to the understorey to mate.

ABOVE: *An Eyelash Viper (*Bothriechis schlegelii*) sits on a heliconia bract waiting to ambush passing prey.*

By far the most numerous animals in the rainforests are the invertebrates, of which well over 200,000 species are estimated to live in the rainforests of Costa Rica. Nesting colonies of hundreds of thousands of leaf-cutter ants (*Atta* and *Acromyrmex* spp.) and army ants of the species *Eciton burchelli* send out their workers to forage over large tracts of forest floor and up into the trees.

In addition, a multitude of cicadas calls in unison from the canopy layer, and more than 1,000 species of butterfly live out their brief but crucial existence here. Some of these butterflies are the size of small birds; the wingspans of both the iridescent Blue Morpho (*Morpho peleides*) and the Cream Owl Butterfly (*Caligo memnon*) can reach an impressive 15 cm.

Countless beetles, caterpillars, web-building spiders and grasshoppers show off a whole spectrum of colours that can be seen from forest trails, and a closer inspection of decomposing logs and hollow trees reveals scorpions, millipedes, yet more beetles and such delights as the 8 cm-long Giant Cockroach (*Blaberus giganteus*).

CONSERVATION

A relatively large proportion of the remaining rainforests in Costa Rica is now enclosed within government- or private-owned protected areas, and the rise in popularity of eco-tourism in Costa Rica over the last fifteen years has played a crucial role in achieving this. However, although the rate of deforestation across the country has reduced significantly in the last ten years, illegal logging inside protected areas and the clearing of forest for agricultural purposes still continues.

To conserve the rainforests in Costa Rica and the wildlife that lives within them, the problem of illegal logging and poaching must be resolved, and the network of forests that exist needs to be better connected with biological corridors to effectively increase their size. Many birds and large mammals need access to sizeable areas of forest in which to find all of the food they require, which is frequently only available during certain seasons.

In addition, larger habitats help to prevent the isolation of small populations and the inbreeding that results. There are many biological corridor projects already under way in different areas of Costa Rica, and they serve as an example of what can be achieved.

On the Osa Peninsula, the Friends of the Osa organization spearheads the Corcovado–Matapalo Biological Corridor. Nearby in Coto Brus, the Organization for Tropical Studies is developing a corridor between its Las Cruces Biological Station and the Guaymi indigenous reserve to the west. In the north-west of the country, the Ministry of the Environment and Energy (MINAE) is working with locals to improve the natural corridor between Tortuguero National Park and Barra del Colorado Wildlife Refuge.

CLOUD FORESTS

The wild upper reaches of much of Costa Rica's continental divide are covered with tropical cloud forests that often disappear from view. Clouds drift through the canopy, swathing the forest in blankets of mist and fine rain. When the sky does clear, rays of sunlight shine through gaps in the treetops to illuminate patches of a damp and dripping understorey below.

This enchanting landscape is decorated with giant ferns and moss-covered, epiphyte-laden trees. One of its greatest attractions to visitors is the opportunity to spot a Resplendant Quetzal (*Pharomachrus mocinno*) or Three-wattled Bellbird (*Procnias tricarunculata*), two of the most sought-after birds in Costa Rica.

GEOGRAPHY AND CLIMATE

Cloud forests blanket many of Costa Rica's upper mountain slopes in a series of protected areas. The most northerly cloud forests surround the Orosi Volcano in Guanacaste National Park near the Nicaraguan border, and the neighbouring Rincón de la Vieja Volcano that sits in its own national park. To the south-east lie the cloud forests of the world-famous Monteverde Cloud Forest Preserve and then Póas, Braulio Carrillo, Irazú and Turrialba National Parks, which surround the Central Valley. Further south there are significant areas of

BELOW: *The cool cloud forests of Braulio Carrillo National Park grow up to an altitude of almost 3,000 m.*

cloud forest on the Cerro de la Muerte mountains and in the national parks of Tapanti, Chirripó and La Amistad.

In Costa Rica, cloud forests grow between altitudes of about 1,000 m and 3,200 m. The clouds that envelop them are formed on the Caribbean slope as winds from the Atlantic Ocean blow warm, humid air up from the lowlands. This air then condenses when it reaches the higher, cooler altitudes and creates a lot of precipitation; most cloud forests in Costa Rica receive over 3 m of rainfall per year as well as moisture directly from the clouds. This water drains into the soil and travels underground before eventually rising to the surface as springs of clean, filtered water lower down the mountainside. In this manner cloud forests store a great deal of water in the ground beneath them, and act as reservoirs for terrain at lower elevations by slowly releasing it throughout both the rainy and dry seasons.

The strong north-easterly winds that bluster across the continental divide have a dramatic effect on the vegetation along the ridgeline and on the upper Caribbean slope. The trees are much shorter than in the more sheltered regions of the cloud forest and their branches grow bent over by the relentless winds. These exposed, wooded areas are known as elfin forests and they are almost always shrouded in swirling mist. There is a beautiful and easily accessible example of this vegetation at the end of the Bosque Nuboso trail in the Monteverde Cloud Forest Preserve.

THE FOREST

To stroll through a misty tropical cloud forest is to feel part of a fairytale. Giant tree ferns stand more than 15 m above the trail, long, arching bamboos crown the tangled understorey vegetation and at night, bioluminescent fungi glow in the darkness. Probably the most striking difference from other types of tropical forest is the extreme proliferation of epiphytic plants that adorn the tree trunks and branches. Thick, spongy moss, bright red and green bromeliads, dangling ferns and ornate orchids compete for space on the crowded bark. In the Monteverde Cloud Forest Preserve there are over 870 different species of such plant living on the trees.

These crowds of epiphytes obtain their water from the surface of the host tree or from the tiny pools that accumulate between their own leaves. Their roots are very short because their principal function is to firmly anchor the plant onto the surface of the tree, rather than dig deep into the earth as is the case with most terrestrial plants.

Some species of epiphytic plant produce roots that gradually grow down to the forest floor and penetrate the soil. They then continue their lives in the manner of terrestrial plants, extracting water and nutrients from the earth. They are known

LEFT: *The view upwards inside a strangler fig. The original host tree that it enveloped has long since died and decomposed.*

as hemi-epiphytes, and probably the best-documented species are the strangler figs. The roots of these figs cling to the trunk of the host tree as they wind downwards, joining with each other to create a mesh of suffocating limbs that eventually arrest the growth of the host. In addition, the leaves of the strangler begin to compete for light with those of the host, leading to the death of the latter. Years later, after the host tree has rotted away, the fig and its multiple roots remain as a fully grown tree.

The weight of epiphytes and the rainwater they hold can sometimes cause the affected tree branch to break off, bringing all of the plants crashing to the forest floor. The result is a light gap in the forest canopy, where the sun's rays can penetrate down to the understorey. An even larger hole is created when the high winds that sweep over the central divide blow an entire tree over, which may even take other trees with it. The saplings on the ground below suddenly receive much more

LEFT: *The pokeweed species* Phytolacca rivinoides *thrives in light gaps on the cloud forest floor.*
BELOW: *The boughs of many cloud forest trees are crowded with bromeliads that provide refuges for insects, amphibians and reptiles.*

light than normal and their growth accelerates as they compete with other plants to occupy a space in the canopy. The pokeweed species *Phytolacca rivinoides* is commonly found in light gaps in the cloud forest. Its seeds are dispersed by birds and, if they are dropped onto soil that is shaded by an unbroken canopy, the seeds can lie dormant for up to 20 or 30 years until a light gap is formed to allow them to germinate.

Bromeliads

The slender, pointed leaves of epiphytic bromeliads form a rosette with their bases, which overlap so tightly that rainfall collects between them and does not leak out. This body of water is enriched with nutrients from the decomposition of leaves that fall into it. These mini-pools provide homes to scores of micro-organisms, which are fed upon by small insects and their larvae. The waste products of these animals, and indeed their bodies when they die, provide additional nutrients to the water that the plant absorbs. The relationship between the bromeliad and its inhabitants is therefore a symbiotic one, where both organisms benefit from each other. Larger, nocturnal animals such as katydids, wolf spiders, scorpions and even snakes can be found hiding in these arboreal communities during the day. Many frogs lay their eggs in the dark and wet interiors of bromeliads. One example is the Highland Tink Frog (*Eleutherodactylus hylaeformis*), which takes refuge in bromeliads during the day and emerges at night to produce one of the most common nocturnal sounds in the forest. Its call is a single '*tink!*' that echoes around the forest, making the frog extremely difficult to locate. The offspring of this species hatch as tiny froglets that feed and grow within the safety of the bromeliad.

At lower elevations, poison arrow frogs carry their newly hatched tadpoles from the floor of the forest to water-filled bromeliads, where they gradually develop into adults.

Orchids

Possibly the largest family of plants in the world is Orchidaceae – the orchid family. Around 25,000 species have been identified worldwide and of these, approximately 1,400 grow naturally in Costa Rica. These plants thrive in the moist cloud forest environment and 420 species are found in the

BELOW: *The Spotted Ponthieva Orchid (*Ponthieva maculata*) is pollinated by flies that seem to be attracted by its spotted petals.*

Monteverde Cloud Forest Preserve alone. Included are the hairy Spotted Ponthieva (*Ponthieva maculata*) and one of the world's smallest orchids, *Platystele jungermannioides*, which stands just 20 mm high and has 1 mm-long sepals.

The orchid family is distinguished by its enormous variety of flower structures, though they all possess the same basic design of three sepals and three petals. One of the petals is modified into a colourful and ornate shape that attracts pollinators, as well as functioning as a landing pad when those pollinators are insects. This petal is called the labellum, or lip, and is the most characteristic part of the flower. Many orchids do not produce nectar, and their elaborate colours and design or sweet scents are simply a trick. By the time a visiting bird or insect discovers there is no nectar, it has already picked up pollen from the flower or deposited pollen that it carried from a different flower.

THE FAUNA

To many visitors, a cloud forest can seem less 'busy' than a lowland rainforest, with fewer sights and sounds of animals. This is partly due to the density of the vegetation, which makes it difficult to see very far, and partly because of the higher elevation, which supports less life. However, green vegetation and fruit is available all year round in a cloud forest, so even though the fauna is not as noticeable, it is still immensely rich and varied.

The tracks of large, terrestrial mammals such as the Baird's Tapir, Puma, Collared Peccary and Red Brocket Deer can be found well preserved in the soft mud of forest trails even though these animals are seldom actually seen. White-faced Capuchins, Spider Monkeys and Mantled Howler Monkeys are more commonly encountered and are easily detected as they swing and jump between branches. Hoffmann's Two-toed and Brown-throated Three-toed Sloths also both inhabit the canopy.

Many smaller cloud forest mammals are active at night. The Olingo (*Bassaricyon gabbii*) and Kinkajou (*Potos flavus*), both related to raccoons, scurry from one treetop to another foraging for fruits, flowers and small invertebrates. Both the Mexican Mouse Opossum (*Marmosa mexicana*) and the Woolly Opossum (*Caluromys derbianus*) can also be spotted as they hang from branches by their prehensile tails, sipping nectar from flowers or picking insects from the bark of a tree. The Grey Fox (*Urocyon cinereoargenteus*), which hunts both on the ground and in trees, will sometimes sit placidly for a few

ABOVE, LEFT: *The tiny* Platystele jungermannioides *orchid is barely visible on the cloud forest trees on which it grows.*
LEFT: *A Purple-throated Mountaingem (*Lampornis calolaema*) feeds on the orchid* Elleanthus glaucophyllus.
OPPOSITE: *The Olingo (*Bassaricyon gabbii*) forages for flowers, fruits and invertebrates in the cloud forest canopy at night.*

moments when illuminated by torchlight before disappearing into the darkness. Mice, shrews, the Paca (*Agouti paca*) – a large rodent – and the Nine-banded Armadillo (*Dasypus novemcinctus*) are also active on the forest floor at night, and an astonishing sixty species of bat patrol the air. Many of these nocturnal mammals can be located with the use of a torch. When they look into a beam of light, the retinas at the backs of their eyes reflect a coloured glow that stands out clearly from the surrounding vegetation.

For ornithologists the cloud forest represents a true paradise. Visitors travel to Costa Rica from around the world to catch a glimpse of the magnificent male Resplendent Quetzal, with its bright green and red plumage and long, trailing tail feathers. The cloud forest is also inhabited by such beautiful species as the Three-wattled Bellbird, the Emerald Toucanet (*Aulacorhynchus prasinus*) and the Golden-browed Chlorophonia (*Chlorophonia callophrys*). One unforgettable sound that carries through the mist is the call of the Black-faced Solitaire (*Myadestes melanops*). The song of this small black thrush is remarkably similar to that of a squeaky shop sign swinging slowly in the wind. The long, drawn-out notes add to the already eerie atmosphere of the misty cloud forest.

Twenty species of hummingbird spend at least part of the year in Costa Rica's cloud forests, where they play the very important role of pollinators to many different plants. The vibrantly coloured Violet Sabrewing, the Purple-throated Mountaingem (*Lampornis calolaema*) and the Green-crowned Brilliant (*Heliodoxa jacula*) are all very common throughout the forested highlands.

While most cloud forest birds migrate during the year to the lowlands or to other countries, more than 10 per cent of the bird species found in Costa Rica's cloud forests are endemic to the Costa Rican and Panamanian highlands. The pheasant-like Black Guan (*Chamaepetes unicolor*) is one common example. This bird is nick-named the 'machine gun' by guides because of the loud crackling sound it produces with its wings when it flies from one perch to another.

More than 100 reptile and amphibian species live in Costa Rica's cloud forests, including transparent glass frogs and poisonous vipers. Twenty years ago this number was significantly higher, but in 1988 many species of frog suddenly and mysteriously began to disappear, including the Golden Toad (*Bufo periglenes*) and the Harlequin Frog (*Atelopus senex*). Neither has been seen for many years and they are now feared extinct. Some species of lizard and snake have also become less common in the cloud forests

ABOVE: *A male Resplendent Quetzal (*Pharomachrus mocinno*) pauses outside its nest-hole before entering with food for its chicks.*
OPPOSITE: *The highest elevations of Monteverde Cloud Forest Preserve are almost always shrouded in mist.*
BELOW: *The Jumping Pit Viper (*Atropoides nummifer*) is one of several venomous snakes that inhabit Costa Rica's cloud forests.*

ABOVE: *A Redleg Tarantula (*Brachypelma emilia*) waits to pounce on prey that passes the entrance to its cloud forest burrow.*
OPPOSITE: *The shrouds of mist that typically cover a cloud forest canopy may suddenly give way to a clear sky and sunshine.*

(*Megaphobema mesomelas*) that lives within.

CONSERVATION

The most serious threat to the cloud forests of Costa Rica is that of deforestation. Cloud forests continue to be cleared for agriculture and when this occurs it has serious consequences for the forests on the foothills below.

Once the cloud forest has been converted into agricultural farmland or an urban development, the water-holding capacity of the land is severely reduced. This results in rainfall flowing down the mountain much faster, which leads to floods in the lowlands after heavy rains and drought during periods of no rainfall. In addition, the chemical pesticides and fertilizers that a farmer uses at the top of the mountain will gradually contaminate all the land below.

Also, the cutting down of lowland rainforest appears to directly affect cloud forests on the mountain slopes above them. When lowland forest on the upwind side of a cloud forest is destroyed, the air temperature rises slightly. This results in warmer air blowing up the mountain slopes, which in turn means that clouds are not formed until slightly higher elevations than before. The lower reaches of cloud forests therefore experience a change in the local climate, which in turn leads to the disappearance of some of the local flora and fauna.

The existence of biological corridors from high-elevation cloud forests down to low-elevation rainforests and dry forests is essential for the survival of many animals that migrate between them. Many fruit-eating birds that breed in the cloud forest, such as the Resplendent Quetzal and the Three-wattled Bellbird, migrate to lower-elevation rainforest after the nesting season, where they can find more fruits during the rainy months of July to November.

Some biological corridors still exist, while others are being re-created by groups such as the Friends of Monteverde Cloud Forest Preserve. This non-profit organization is using private donations to piece together a continuous strip of land between Monteverde and the Nicoya Peninsula. It has already purchased a significant area of land from local farmers, but unfortunately faces competition from both hotels and property developers.

in recent years and scientists are puzzled as to the cause. Theories put forward to explain their scarcity include global warming, air pollution and viruses.

The number of insect and arachnid species that inhabit the cloud forests of Costa Rica is enormous. Tens of thousands have been recorded and no doubt there are many more that have yet to be discovered. During the day and especially when it is sunny, Glasswing (Ithomiinae) and Morpho (Morphinae) butterflies dance through the air in the understorey as they search for flowers and rotting fruits to feed on. On the tree trunks and in the leaf litter roam beetles including the world's largest, the Hercules Beetle (*Dynastes hercules*), and species of shiny, metallic golden beetles (e.g. *Chrysina aurigans*). Praying mantises lurk in the vegetation waiting to snare passing insects with their spiny forelegs, and the yellow and black Python Millipede (*Nyssodesmus python*) glides its way across the ground. At dusk, long, hairy legs appear at the entrance holes of dark burrows in the cloud forest floor. Any large insect or even a small rodent that passes too close is likely to be snatched off its feet by the Orange-kneed Tarantula

DRY FORESTS

Tropical dry forests are most unlike the dark and misty rainforests and cloud forests that we normally associate with a tropical wilderness. For almost six months of each year the dry forests receive virtually no rainfall, which results in an arid landscape of leafless trees and bone-dry earth shimmering under a merciless sun. The temperature regularly rises to above 30°C during the day. Once the annual rains bring an end to the prolonged dry season, this ecosystem bursts into life with an explosion of animal and plant activity. Just weeks after the first raindrops patter over the parched hillsides and valleys, a canopy of green, white and yellow treetops once again shadows the dry forest floor.

GEOGRAPHY AND CLIMATE

Until the early 19th century there was an unbroken band of tropical dry forest that ran from Mexico to the central Pacific coast of Costa Rica. Since then, however, that strip has become drastically fragmented due to farming, timber extraction and fires. As a consequence, dry forest is presently much rarer than rainforest in the region. There are probably no more than 2,500 sq km of dry forest remaining in Costa Rica. This area is made up of a number of smaller, separated areas, almost all of which have been logged, burned or farmed at some time in the past.

These patches of forest grow in the north-west lowlands of the country from the Nicaraguan border down to the River Tárcoles on the central Pacific coast.

The principal national parks and reserves where dry forest is found are Santa Rosa, Guanacaste, Palo Verde, Barra Honda and Lomas de Barbudal (see page 158). The terrain is quite flat in these protected areas, with small hills that rise no more than a few hundred metres above sea level. Many of these slightly higher elevations include rocky limestone summits that were originally coral reefs when the ocean covered this land some 50 million years ago. These reefs were gradually raised above sea level by the shifting of the region's continental plates.

Dry forests exist in this region and nowhere else in Costa Rica because of the unique local climate. From December to April trade winds blow across Costa Rica from the Caribbean Sea. This warm air is forced upwards by the central mountain range and then cools before releasing its moisture as rainfall. Most of this precipitation falls on the mountains before the wind reaches the north-west of the country. The winds reaching Guanacaste are therefore usually very low in moisture and so produce very little rain. In May the trade winds move north, allowing winds to blow in from the Pacific Ocean, which carry moisture from the sea and cause more rainfall on the lowlands of the west coast.

THE FOREST

The vegetation of a tropical dry forest is typically layered into just two levels: a canopy and an understorey. The canopy is composed of mostly deciduous trees that average between 10 and 15 m in height, though some species tower to 30 m or more. One fine example is the national tree of Costa Rica, the Guanacaste (*Enterolobium cyclocarpum*). Within the forest mature trees of this species can grow to 35 m in height even though their outward growth can be somewhat restricted by the surrounding trees. On farmland, however, they can grow outwards to their full potential over the open space, taking the form of a gigantic umbrella. Other distinct canopy species include the Cannonball Tree (*Couroupita nicaraguarensis*), which grows melon-sized fruits, the Chicle Tree (*Manilkara*

OPPOSITE: *The Guanacaste Tree (*Enterolobium cyclocarpum*) quickly produces new leaves when the first rains begin in April.*
BELOW: *The Ant Acacia (*Acacia collinsii*) has large thorns and a resident colony of aggressive ants that protect it from herbivores.*

chicle), which produces sticky latex, and the precious and endangered Ronrón (*Astronium graveolens*) and Rosewood (*Dalbergia retusa*) hardwood trees.

On the boughs of the canopy trees there are very few epiphytes, which is in strong contrast to the bromeliad-laden branches of rainforest and cloud forest trees. This is because in a dry forest it is difficult for the trees to acquire and maintain enough moisture and nutrients on their exposed canopy branches during the hot, dry season.

The understorey consists of a tangle of Monkey Ladder vines, small thorny trees, cacti and spiky-leaved shrubs.

The Ant Acacia (*Acacia collinsii*) is a small tree that is one of the most prevalent species in the dry forest understorey. Its success is largely due to the mutually beneficial (mutualistic) relationship that it has with different species of acacia ant (*Pseudomyrmex* spp.). These insects live protected from predators inside the stem and bulbous thorns of the Ant Acacia. They feed on sugar from extrafloral nectaries and protein from small, yellow Beltian bodies on the leaves (named after British naturalist Thomas Belt, who studied this relationship in the 19th century). They also patrol the ground around the base of the tree and destroy any emerging seedlings that would eventually compete with their host plant for water, nutrients and light. As a result, in the dry forest there are large areas of bare forest floor from which only acacia plants and large trees can be seen growing.

Almost any animal that comes into contact with the Ant Acacia is received by a host of biting ants and quickly repelled. However, there are some exceptions: the Streak-backed Oriole (*Icterus pustulatus*), Great Kiskadee (*Pitangus sulphuratus*) and Rufous-naped Wren (*Campylorhynchus rufinucha*) are all birds that build their nests in Ant Acacias and are curiously left unmolested by the host ants once the ants have become familiar with the new nest material. The Ant Acacia Beetle (*Pelidnota punctulata*) also seems immune to the aggressive behaviour of the acacia ants. This insect feeds exclusively on the Ant Acacia and happily grazes on the plant's leaves while the resident ants swarm over it, trying in vain to bite through the beetle's hard exoskeleton.

Two species of cacti, *Stenocereus aragonii* and *Acanthocereus tetragonus*, are very common in the tropical dry forests of north-west Costa Rica. Both are tall, thin plants that grow to several metres in length. However, they grow in

ABOVE: *The Rufous-naped Wren (*Campylorhynchus rufinucha*) is one of a small number of birds that builds its nests on the Ant Acacia and is remarkably not attacked by the resident ants.*
LEFT: *A Streak-backed Oriole (*Icterus pustulatus*) sits at the entrance to its almost-completed nest in an Ant Acacia plant.*

very different ways. While *S. aragonii* extends straight upwards towards the sky, *A. tetragonus* grows in huge loops that sprawl across the ground. In contrast to most other plants in the dry forest, cacti actually achieve most of their growth during the dry season. There are two reasons for this: firstly they require large amounts of direct sunlight to grow well, and secondly they are well equipped to cope with the arid conditions of this period. During the dry season, there is much less shade from neighbouring trees, most of which have shed their leaves, so the cacti receive a lot more light. The lack of water in the dry season is usually not a problem for cacti because inside their stems they are able to store a large amount of water, collected mainly at the end of the rainy season. This water is gradually released through the plant over the dry months that follow.

THE FAUNA

The number of animal species found in a tropical dry forest is usually lower than that of a neighbouring tropical rainforest of

the same area. During the dry season the dry forest can have up to 50 per cent fewer species than the rainforest. There is, however, still plenty of life to see, and the variety of behaviour employed by different species to cope with the radically different seasons is quite fascinating.

The most commonly seen mammals are the Mantled Howler Monkey, White-faced Capuchin, White-tailed Deer (*Odocoileus virginianus*), White-nosed Coati, Central American Agouti (*Dasyprocta punctata*), Variegated Squirrel (*Sciurus variegatoides*) and Collared Peccary. All of these species are active during the day and are quite easy to encounter around waterholes and trees that are producing fruit. Other, more elusive mammals include the Baird's Tapir, Northern Tamandua, Spider Monkey, Puma, Ocelot (*Leopardus pardalis*), Grey Fox and Mexican Hairy Porcupine (*Coendou mexicanus*). In Costa Rica some species of mammal are found only in the dry north-west; these include the Virginia Opossum (*Didelphis virginiana*), Hooded Skunk (*Mephitis macroura*) and Gray Sac-winged Bat (*Balantiopteryx plicata*).

Bird species are numerous in the dry forests. On the forest floor walk the well-camouflaged Thicket Tinamou (*Crypturellus cinnamomeus*) and majestic Great Curassow (*Crax rubra*). A wealth of species can be found in the trees, including the

ABOVE: *On an unusually misty morning in the dry forest, a Variegated Squirrel (*Sciurus variegatoides*) gnaws at new buds.*
OPPOSITE, ABOVE LEFT: *The Black-headed Trogon (*Trogon melanocephalus*) flyies sorties to snatch insects and fruits from trees.*
OPPOSITE, ABOVE RIGHT: *The White-throated Magpie-Jay (*Calocitta formosa*) is one of the most common dry forest birds.*
OPPOSITE, BOTTOM: *The Turquoise-browed Motmot (*Eumomota superciliosa*) is often near the ground where it builds its nest.*

Turquoise-browed Motmot (*Eumomota superciliosa*), White-throated Magpie-Jay (*Calocitta formosa*), Black-headed Trogon (*Trogon melanocephalus*), Mangrove Cuckoo (*Coccyzus minor*), Ferruginous Pygmy-Owl (*Glaucidium brasilianum*) and flycatchers and orioles. The brightly coloured Plain-capped Starthroat (*Heliomaster constantii*) and Cinnamon Humming-bird (*Amazilia rutila*) are very much at home in the north-west lowlands of Costa Rica; they are seen here more than any-where else in the country. Several parrot species are extremely conspicuous in the area – the Yellow-naped Parrot (*Amazona auropalliata*) and White-fronted Parrot (*Amazona albifrons*) reg-ularly announce their presence with a cacophony of squawks. There also remain a few mating pairs of the endangered Scarlet Macaw in the dry forest of Palo Verde National Park.

ABOVE: *The Central American Coral Snake (*Micrurus nigrocinctus*) hunts mainly other snakes among the leaf litter of the forest floor.* OPPOSITE, ABOVE: *The well-camouflaged Green Iguana (*Iguana iguana*) is Costa Rica's largest lizard, growing to over 1.5 m long.* OPPOSITE, BELOW: *The Black and White Cat-eyed Snake (*Leptodeira nigrofasciata*) hunts frogs and small lizards at night.*

The hot climate of the dry north-west lowlands provides an ideal home for a variety of different reptiles. Indeed, several species of snake, such as the Neotropical Rattlesnake (*Crotalus durissus*), Scorpion-eater (*Stenorrhina freminvillii*) and Black-and-White Cat-eyed Snake (*Leptodeira nigrofasciata*), are found in no other region of Costa Rica. The Boa Constrictor and Central American Coral Snake (*Micrurus nigrocinctus*) are

two easily recognized snakes that also inhabit the region.

The two largest species of lizard found in Costa Rica, the Green Iguana (*Iguana iguana*) and Black Spiny-tailed Iguana (*Ctenosaura similis*), are common here, and the smaller but much more active Central American Whip-tailed Lizard (*Ameiva festiva*) is frequently heard rustling in the leaf litter. The Red-cheeked Mud Turtle (*Kinosternon scorpioides*) lives near water, but during the height of the dry season will bury itself under the ground until the rains return.

Few amphibians live in the dry forests of Costa Rica because most species' skin is thin and permeable to water, so that they dehydrate extremely quickly in hot and dry conditions. The Dry Forest Toad (*Bufo coccifer*) and Cane Toad (*Bufo marinus*) are two exceptions to this general rule because they

have very thick skin that significantly reduces water loss from the body. Both species maintain large populations in the north-west. Thousands of insect and spider species inhabit the region, and this number increases significantly at the beginning of the rainy season, when a large number of flying insects return from their temporary migration to surrounding evergreen forests. Butterflies like the Julia Butterfly (*Dyras julia*) and Malachite Butterfly (*Siproeta stelenes biplagiata*), ants, wasps and bees are probably the most commonly seen insects during a walk in the forest, though a little more investigation reveals many others. Zebra Tarantulas (*Aphonopelma seemanni*) sit patiently at the entrances to their tunnels at dusk, caterpillars emerge in huge numbers at the beginning of the wet season and can be found munching on the undersides of leaves, while leaf-coloured praying mantises and grasshoppers blend with the dried vegetation on the ground.

ABOVE: *A Malachite Butterfly (*Siproeta stelenes biplagiata*) dries its wings in the early morning light.*
BELOW: *A Gumbo Limbo Tree (*Bursera simaruba*) begins to flower at the beginning of the wet season.*

THE CYCLE OF SEASONS

The annual rainfall in tropical dry forests averages between 1 and 2 m, most of which falls between May and November. By the end of the wet season in December, these forests are lush with green vegetation following months of precipitation. Many trees still flower and the ground is humid with high levels of bacterial and fungal activity in the leaf litter. The canopy and understorey are full of young mammals, birds and reptiles that were born during the wet months when food was much more abundant.

Once the dry season begins in earnest, sunshine and clear blue skies replace the afternoon clouds and rainstorms. In turn, the trees react to this change in the daily weather pattern by halting the production of fruit and by having short flowering periods that are synchronized between trees of the same species. Most also begin to shed their leaves, and by doing so these plants can drastically reduce the surface area from which they lose water through transpiration. If they were to keep their leaves during the dry season, they would lose far more water than they could obtain from the ground and in many cases the consequences would be fatal.

When a plant drops its leaves it usually loses most or all of the green chlorophyll pigment that it requires to photosynthesize. This means that energy production and therefore growth stop until new leaves are produced at the beginning of the following rainy season. However, some species have large amounts of chlorophyll in the outer layer of their trunk and branches that allow them to continue photosynthesizing and growing even when they don't have leaves. The most noticeable of these in the Costa Rican dry forests are the Gumbo Limbo Tree (*Bursera simaruba*) and Palo Verde Tree (*Parkinsonia aculeata*). The limbs of both species are a medium-green colour and on the Gumbo Limbo Tree this is contrasted beautifully with the older red-brown bark that peels off the tree like sunburnt skin (lending the species its nickname of 'tourist tree'). Cacti are other examples of plants that use their stems for photosynthesis in order to compensate for the absence of leaves.

ABOVE: *The Gumbo Limbo Tree's (*Bursera simaruba*) trunk contains chlorophyll, so it can photosynthesize even with no leaves.*

The oak species *Quercus oleoides* is one of the dry forest evergreen trees that keeps its leaves during the dry season and has special adaptations to combat the scarcity of water. Its leaves have a thick, waxy cuticle to reduce water loss. Modified tissues in the stem and roots store water after heavy rain, and its roots penetrate deep into the ground to provide the plant with water even when the topsoil has dried out. Several species, such as the Ant Acacia, fold their leaves shut at night to reduce transpiration, a process called nyctinasty.

eat mainly tougher and slightly more toxic mature leaves during the dry months. Peccaries also adopt a less savoury diet when the forest dries up, surviving on vines, tubers and roots instead of the more tasty fruits and seeds that can be found at other times of the year.

Some species of insect, amphibian and reptile simply hide away and sleep through the harshest period of the dry season. The Mexican Burrowing Toad (*Rhinophrynus dorsalis*) is one. It uses its spade-like hind feet to dig itself under the ground, where it remains buried alive for up to a month or more at a time. During this period the animal enters a state of summer hibernation, called aestivation. To prevent dehydration, its metabolism slows down greatly, which means less water is used for its bodily functions. Individuals may come out of their chambers to feed on ants and termites on some cool nights during the dry season, and at the beginning of the rainy season there is a simultaneous, mass emergence of these toads. As soon as the water from the first heavy rainstorm seeps into their burrows, the toads emerge into the night and congregate around newly formed ponds to mate.

ABOVE: *Hundreds of Mexican Burrowing Toads (*Rhinophrynus dorsalis*) leave their burrows with the first rainy season downpour.* OPPOSITE: *The Yellow Cortéz Tree (*Tabebuia ochracea*) bursts into flower at the beginning of the rainy season.*

Evergreen species must also have very good defences against herbivores if they are to survive the dry season. During this time there are few green plants that plant-eating mammals, lizards and insects can feed on, so those that do remain are much more likely to attract the attention of these animals. Many such plants are armed with thorns and spines; other plants have spiky leaf tips and very unpalatable tissues that help keep herbivores at bay.

The behaviour of animals in a tropical dry forest changes as the dry season begins. The shortage of food and water and the changes in their distribution force many species to alter their diets, travel more extensively, migrate or even bury themselves in the ground and sleep until the rains return.

In the early dry season, many mammals, birds and insects migrate to green, woody areas within the dry forest that surround streams or other bodies of water. These patches of land are called riparian forests, and between December and April their environment is cooler and more humid than elsewhere in the dry forest.

Large mammals such as cats, tapirs and monkeys expand their territories in the early dry season in order to find enough food and water to satisfy their needs. The quality and variety of the food available is often inferior to that of the wet season. Howler Monkeys, for example, which prefer to forage on fruits, flowers and young leaves during the rainy season, are forced to

The First Rains

In April or May the first heavy rains bring the months of heat and dryness to an abrupt end. Within days, green leaves and fruits appear in the previously bare canopy. Lifeless, skeletal trunks and branches across the hillsides and valleys are suddenly engulfed by an explosion of colour as their flowers emerge and unfold.

The Rain Tree (*Albizia saman*) produces fan-like pink and white flowers, while the Palo Verde Tree has dense yellow and red blooms and the Rosewood tree decorates itself with a mass of white petals. The bright yellow Cortéz Tree (*Tabebuia ochracea*), however, is probably the most vibrant of all the dry forest flowering trees. Its bloom of cartwheel-shaped flowers lasts for about four days, during which time the tree is visited by swarms of bees that hover among the branches, pollinating the flowers.

The dry forest is suddenly alive and active once again. Plants rapidly produce chlorophyll-rich green leaves that can photosynthesize and provide them with the energy to resume growth. Water in the leaf litter causes an explosion of activity in bacteria and tiny insects that decompose fallen leaves and branches, releasing nutrients that are finally returned to the plants through their roots.

An abundance of new food becomes available to the animals living in the forest and those that return from their seasonal refuges in nearby evergreen riparian forests or rainforests.

New leaves and fruits are eaten by monkeys, tapirs, bats, iguanas, numerous species of bird, caterpillars, ants and crickets. The pollen of blooming flowers attracts animals such as butterflies, bees and hummingbirds. Many animals reproduce at this time to ensure that their offspring are born during the wet season, when there is still plenty of food and water in the forest. This is very evident in birds, whose nests appear throughout the forest in April, with mating pairs flying countless sorties, bringing back grass and twigs to complete their new homes.

During the months that follow, the animals and plants of the tropical dry forest exploit the ready supply of water to the maximum as they grow and reproduce in preparation for yet another period of drought.

CONSERVATION

Most of the little remaining tropical dry forest in Costa Rica is now legally protected within a handful of national parks and reserves. In addition, there have been initiatives aimed at recovering surrounding areas of private land and using them to increase the size of this protected wilderness. The Guanacaste

ABOVE: *The beginning of another scorching hot day in the dry forest of Palo Verde National Park.*

Dry Forest Conservation Fund, which was set up by world-famous biologist and conservationist Professor Daniel Janzen of North America's University of Pennsylvania, has been purchasing land from willing local owners for several years now. The newly acquired land contains large tracts of rainforest that provide the dry forest animals with an important dry-season refuge.

To ensure that protected areas of dry forest are kept safe they need to be well managed and patrolled. The greatest threats to their existence come from fires, hunting and illegal timber extraction.

During the dry season, fires spread extremely easily and quickly through the desiccated vegetation, and are fanned on by strong winds. The majority of the fires are started by humans, either by accident or as reprisals carried out by resentful hunters or loggers. In late March 2007, for example, approximately 18 sq km of regenerating dry forest in Guanacaste National Park was severely damaged by a fire of human origin. However, despite events such as these, the amount of dry forest in Costa Rica affected by fire has reduced significantly over the last ten years as a result of preventative measures and awareness campaigns.

FRESHWATER MARSHES

The congregation of waterbirds on a Costa Rican freshwater marsh can be a very crowded and noisy affair. By the beginning of the dry season there are tens of thousands of birds feeding within a few square kilometres of open land. Ducks, spoonbills, ibises, egrets, herons and Jabirús (Jabiru mycteria) probe the shallow waters for fish, snails, insects, molluscs and seeds; clouds of bright green dragonflies skim and dance over the surface of the lagoon, and everything is watched by the sharp eyes of Spectacled Caimans (Caiman crocodilus) lying hidden and still, just below the surface of the water.

The torrential downpours of the rainy season from May to December change much of the Costa Rican landscape, and nowhere are those changes more obvious than on the flood-plains of the Río Tempisque in Guanacaste and the Río Frío close to the northern border with Nicaragua. These are the most important seasonal freshwater marshes in the country and possibly even in Central America. In 1991 the Costa Rican government officially registered them on the Ramsar List of Wetlands of International Importance.

Once the rains begin in earnest, the overflow from the rivers in both locations, as well as the accumulation of rain-water on the land, result in the flooding of large areas of open countryside. The floods attract resident birds from around Costa Rica and migrating species from both North and South America.

BELOW: *Thousands of Black-bellied Whistling Ducks (Dendrocygna autumnalis) winter around the lagoon in Palo Verde National Park.*

On the northern bank of the Río Tempisque – the river that gradually widens to become the Gulf of Nicoya – a significant portion of this flooded area is protected within Palo Verde National Park. A shallow lake in this park grows to several square kilometres in size during the floods. Part of the Río Frío watershed is also contained within a protected area; the Caño Negro National Wildlife Refuge has a seasonal lagoon that reaches a size of 8 sq km by the end of the rainy season. Huge flocks of resident and migrant birds feed in these wetland areas between October and March. Over sixty species have been recorded on and around the waters of the Palo Verde lagoon, and a similar number inhabit the waters of Caño Negro.

Groups of more than 20,000 Black-bellied Whistling Ducks (*Dendrocygna autumnalis*) assemble to forage in the shallows, and Blue-winged Teal (*Anas discors*), Wood Storks (*Mycteria americana*) and Cattle Egrets (*Bubulcus ibis*) also gather in their hundreds. Adding their own striking colours to these huge mixed flocks are the bright pink Roseate Spoonbill (*Ajaia ajaja*), Purple Gallinule (*Porphyrula martinica*) and brown and yellow Northern Jacana (*Jacana spinosa*), whose shrill alarm call carries far across the water.

The critically endangered Jabirú stork feeds on mud eels and small fish in both the Palo Verde and Caño Negro lagoons, its last remaining sizeable protected habitats in Costa Rica. The White Ibis (*Eudocimus albus*) and Glossy Ibis (*Plegadis falcinellus*) prod the soft mud with their curved bills for hidden frogs and insects, while the very tall Bare-throated Tiger Heron

ABOVE: *A Spectacled Caiman (*Caiman crocodilus*) holds a fish it has caught in the freshwater marsh of Caño Negro Wildlife Refuge.*

(*Tigrisoma mexicanum*) stands perfectly still as it looks down on the water waiting for fish to swim by.

Freshwater marshes also offer some raptors an excellent source of food. The Snail Kite (*Rostrhamus sociabilis*) feasts on large snails that live on the marsh vegetation, and the Osprey (*Pandion haliaetus*) snatches fish from the surface of the water.

In addition, Caño Negro is the nesting ground for up to 400 pairs of Olivaceous Cormorants (*Phalacrocorax olivaceus*), the largest such group in the country. The Río Frío region is also the only place in Costa Rica that is inhabited by the Nicaraguan Grackle (*Quiscalus nicaraguensis*).

Birds share the freshwater marshes of Palo Verde and Caño Negro with several other large animals. The Spectacled Caiman is common and towards the end of the dry season, when the lagoons shrink, many of these crocodilians can be found residing together in small, isolated ponds. The Northern Raccoon (*Procyon lotor*) will visit the water's edge to search for food, and after nightfall the Coyote (*Canis latrans*) stalks small birds around the lagoons. In the Palo Verde lagoon, the Red-cheeked Mud Turtle ambles along the bottom feeding on small invertebrates, where it may flush out frogs that are quickly snapped up by the wading birds above. During the dry season from January to April, the freshwater marshes slowly dry up. By March, huge numbers of wildfowl are gathered around the small remaining lagoons that grow smaller by the day under the heat of the untiring sun. Large areas of dried and cracked mud separate these bodies of water. Over the following weeks the migrant bird species begin their journeys back to temperate climates, and many resident species begin to look elsewhere for food. The flat, muddy plain that remains is uncharacteristically quiet and empty as it gradually begins to collect the rainwater of the new wet season.

CONSERVATION

Even though both the Palo Verde and Caño Negro freshwater marshes are enclosed within the boundaries of state-protected areas, their continued survival, as well as that of other seasonal freshwater marshlands in the Río Frío and Río Tempisque watersheds, is still under threat from agricultural practices in the surrounding countryside. The water discharged from farm irrigation systems carries harmful sediment, loaded with fertilizers and pesticides, into the marshlands. It can also cause flooding during the dry season, which in turn damages invertebrate populations that are dependent on a wet/dry cycle of seasons. Many biologists and conservationists insist that these practices ought to be more closely studied and controlled in order to reduce their destructive effects.

Around the Caño Negro reserve there are a number of privately owned wetlands that are being converted into fields for cattle grazing. Such activity is rapidly isolating Caño Negro and reducing the total number of lagoons where birds can feed.

Several bird species that feed in freshwater marshes are in severe danger of extinction in Costa Rica. The Fulvous Whistling Duck (*Dendrocygna bicolor*), whose nests are destroyed by rice-harvesting machines, and the Jabirú and Roseate Spoonbill all exist in greatly reduced numbers – their future survival will depend on how well the freshwater marshes are preserved.

On a more positive note, the lagoon in Palo Verde National Park has been the subject of a highly successful recent initiative to provide more open water to visiting birds. During the 1980s and '90s there was a rapid increase in the growth of aquatic plants in the lagoon such as the highly invasive Cattail (*Typha domingensis*). The reduced surface area of the lagoon resulted in fewer birds visiting the site and some species, such as the Black-bellied Whistling Duck, began to feed on nearby rice plantations. The growth of the Cattail is usually controlled by the flooding of the marsh during the wet season, but during this period there was less rainfall than normal due to the effects of El Niño. In addition, the flow of water into the lagoon from

ABOVE: *The Bare-throated Tiger Heron (*Tigrisoma mexicanum*) uses its height to survey marshes for its aquatic food.*

one neighbouring watershed was cut off by the construction of an access road to a nearby cattle ranch. The growth of Cattail was also aided by the prohibition of grazing cattle once the area was declared a national park in 1980. In 2001, a joint effort by the Ministry of the Environment and Energy (MINAE), the Organization for Tropical Studies (OTS), the US Wildlife Department and the conservation organization Ducks Unlimited among others, sent teams to physically clear the Cattail from the lagoon area as well as clearing creeks and building dikes to achieve more favourable water levels. Cattle were also allowed back onto the land to graze. By 2007, the scheme was pronounced a total success, with a significant increase in the area of the open lagoon and the biodiversity of the aquatic plants living within it.

BEACHES & MANGROVES

The mainland of Costa Rica is just 464 km long between its most north-westerly and south-easterly points. However, it has almost 1,300 km of tropical beaches, rocky headlands and gaping estuaries along its two coasts. Slightly over 200 km of this coastline faces the Caribbean Sea, and almost 1,100 km forms a boundary with the Pacific Ocean in the west. Tropical rainforest and tropical dry forest form the natural backdrops to the beaches and mangroves that dominate the shoreline, and a host of flora and fauna inhabits these coastal ecosystems, many species having had to evolve distinct physiology and behaviour in order to cope with the harsh environmental conditions.

BEACHES

Most reputable maps of Costa Rica label at least 50 well-known beaches along the coasts, and tucked in between those there is at least the same number again. Though many have been developed for tourism, there still remain a significant number of beaches whose natural states have been preserved and where wildlife abounds.

In the north-west of the country around the Nicoya Peninsula and its Gulf, the Pacific coastline is made up of numerous beaches and bays that are separated and secluded by rocky headlands. The vegetation that overlooks the beaches is mainly that of deciduous tropical dry forest with modest-sized trees, spiny shrubs, grasses and cacti.

Further south, from Carara National Park all the way to the border with Panama, the coastline is less convoluted than in

OPPOSITE: *A deserted beach in Manuel Antonio National Park at first light.*
BELOW: *Large stretches of the Caribbean coast of Costa Rica are bordered by dense rainforest.*

the north-west, with many beaches that extend as far as the eye can see. Beyond the sandy shore lie hills of lush rainforest with dense, evergreen vegetation that contrasts strongly with the dry forest of the north-west.

Most of the Caribbean shore could almost be classed as one long beach; the coastline between the Nicaraguan border and Cahuita National Park (nearly 200 km south) is all but a straight line, interrupted only by a handful of estuaries and the port of Limón. It was on these shores that Christopher Columbus landed in 1502 during his fourth and final voyage to the 'New World'. From Cahuita to the Panamanian border the landscape is much more varied, with many coves and smaller beaches of white, yellow and black sands.

THE FLORA AND FAUNA
Beaches are uninhabitable for most animals and plants; the direct sunlight, heated sand, wave action, salt spray and lack of fresh water prove too severe for the development of most life. However, a small number of species do live in this ecosystem and many more visit to feed.

ABOVE: *A new day breaks in Manuel Antonio National Park.*
OPPOSITE: *Flowers of the Beach Morning Glory (*Ipomoea pes-caprae*), seen here in Tortuguero National Park, open only during the early morning to minimize water loss.*

Many of the plants that live on Costa Rica's beaches also grow naturally in other countries and even on other continents. This is because they have access to a dispersal mechanism that can safely carry their seeds thousands of kilometres from the mother plant: the ocean. Coconut Palm Trees (*Cocos nucifera*) are probably the best-known example. Their hard-cased and buoyant coconuts are perfectly built to survive many months at sea. The Beach Morning Glory (*Ipomoea pes-caprae*) is a creeping vine that is found in the Americas, Africa and Asia. It produces very long stems that extend for several metres across the surface of the sand. The bright pink flowers that bloom from these stems are unmistakable and are a common sight at the top end of beaches on both coasts in Costa Rica. The plant's leaves are thick and waxy to help retain its valuable store of fresh water, and only open in the early morning to avoid expo-

sure to the strong midday sun, which would accelerate water loss. Its seeds are washed from the beach by a high tide.

The Tropical Almond Tree (*Terminalia catappa*) also disperses its seeds around the world on ocean currents and is one of the most attractive beach trees in Costa Rica. Its combination of bright red, orange and green leaves is spectacular and bears close similarity to the autumn tree colours seen in temperate countries. It grows on both coasts, and long strips of these trees line the beaches of the Osa Peninsula, where small flocks of Scarlet Macaws feed enthusiastically on the fleshy fruits.

Not all dangerous organisms in Costa Rica have sharp fangs or a vicious sting. A relatively nondescript tree species found on the country's Pacific beaches is one of the most poisonous plants in the world. The Manchineel Tree (*Hippomane mancinella*) grows to a large size and has boughs that hang low over the sand. While it may provide welcome shade on a sunny day, its fruits, leaves and bark contain a highly toxic latex sap that causes severe irritation or illness if handled or ingested. Because of the poisonous nature of its fruits, seeds of the Manchineel Tree are dispersed exclusively by the sea. An example of this species can be seen just inside the beach entrance to Manuel Antonio National Park.

The animal life on Costa Rica's beaches predominantly comprises species that visit the intertidal zone in search of food or a place to nest. The animals that do reside permanently in the sand are small molluscs and crustaceans, the most commonly seen of which are crabs. Yellow Ghost Crabs (*Ocypode quadrata*), bright red Painted Ghost Crabs (*Ocypode gaudichaudii*) and various species of hermit crab are abundant on Costa Rica's beaches, where they can be seen sifting through the sand close to their burrows, feeding on microscopic organisms.

These crabs, as well as other crustaceans, molluscs, marine worms, insects and fish, are all hunted on the beach, amid the

ABOVE: *Scarlet Macaws (*Ara Macao*) commonly feed on the fruits of the vibrantly coloured Tropical Almond Tree (*Terminalia catappa*).*
OPPOSITE: *Palm Trees (*Cocos nucifera*) have colonized both coastlines of Costa Rica; they thrive in the strong sunlight of the tropics.*

surf and in rock pools, by a host of other, larger animals. The high temperatures and hot sand provide the perfect environment for lizards such as Deppe's Whip-tailed Lizard (*Cnemidophorus deppii*) and the Black Spiny-tailed Iguana,

ABOVE: *The strong jaws of the omnivorous Black Spiny-tailed Iguana (*Ctenosaura similis*) are ideal for crushing its food.*
LEFT: *A Whimbrel (*Numenius phaeopus*) regurgitates shell and sand it ingested while feeding on crustaceans and molluscs on the beach.*

which chase down insects and crabs respectively among the leaf litter at the top of the beach. Closer to the water, sandpipers, Surfbirds (*Aphriza virgata*) and Whimbrels (*Numenius phaeopus*) march busily along the surf pecking and probing the sand and rocks for food. After consuming a number of prey items, they pause to regurgitate pellets of indigestible shell, crab exoskeleton and sand before continuing their exploration. Snowy Egrets (*Egretta thula*) and Yellow-crowned Night Herons (*Nyctanassa violacea*) patrol at a slower pace, carefully inspecting the receding waves for a tumbling shell or stranded fish. Over the breaking waves fly files of Brown Pelicans (*Pelecanus occidentalis*) that stall, tuck in their wings and dive headlong onto unsuspecting shoals of fish.

The trees that overhang the sand are visited by mammals whenever there are flowers, fruits, succulent leaves or insects to eat. Monkeys and squirrels pass through during the day and at night possums, Northern Tamanduas and perhaps the occasional Kinkajou can be seen by torchlight.

ABOVE: *Female Olive Ridley Turtles (*Lepidochelys olivacea*) arrive on Ostional Beach to lay their eggs.*
RIGHT: *Snowy Egrets (*Egretta thula*) search the lower beach in Las Baulas Marine National Park for small fish that wash in with the surf.*

The beaches of Costa Rica are used as nesting grounds by six species of marine turtle, including the world's largest, the Leatherback Turtle (*Dermochelys coriacea*). The Olive Ridley Turtle (*Lepidochelys olivacea*) arrives in by far the largest numbers; during the egg-laying season, the beaches of Ostional and Nancite on the Nicoya Peninsula receive tens of thousands of females in a single night.

The arrival of turtles on a beach and the subsequent hatching of their babies attract a number of predators. Jaguars often migrate to the coast from deep within the forest, tempted by the opportunity of easy, slow-moving prey. Northern Raccoons and White-nosed Coatis dig up eggs from shallow nests, and crabs intercept the hatchlings as they emerge. Black Vultures (*Coragyps atratus*) congregate in large numbers on nesting beaches to feed on the eggs from exposed nests and emerging hatchlings. In turn, their presence attracts Crested Caracaras (*Polyborus plancus*) and Wood Storks, for whom the vultures reluctantly step aside.

MANGROVES

At the mouth of an estuary, where a river flows into the ocean, there is a turbulent zone where fresh and salt waters meet. Twice a day, the high tide pushes against the flow of the river and floods over the adjacent lowland. This terrain is uninhabitable to most plants, though there is a small number of tree species that have evolved to thrive under such conditions. These species form the ecosystem known as mangrove forest or mangrove swamp, and through their hardiness they provide a vital habitat to enormous numbers of land and aquatic animals.

In Costa Rica, mangrove forests are found principally on the Pacific coast where there is a relatively wide intertidal zone for them to grow in. The average rise and fall of the tide is almost 3 m on this coast – on the Caribbean side the difference is ten times less (0.3 m), which doesn't provide enough space for a sizeable mangrove forest to develop. Nevertheless, there are small areas of mangrove in the Gandoca-Manzanillo Wildlife Refuge and along the jungle canals between Limón and Tortuguero National Park. The most extensive mangrove forest in the country can be found on either side of the estuaries of the Rivers Sierpe and Terraba on the south Pacific coast. Other significant areas of mangrove grow in the Tamarindo and Curú Wildlife Refuges on the Nicoya Peninsula, on the Isla de Pájaros in the Gulf of Nicoya, around the mouth of the River Tárcoles on the central Pacific coast and in Marino Ballena National Park to its south.

There are more than fifty mangrove tree species worldwide, and in Costa Rica seven from four different families are represented: red mangroves (Rhizophoraceae), black mangroves (Acanthaceae), tea mangroves (Pellicieraceae) and white mangroves (Combretaceae). The Buttonwood Tree (*Conocarpus erectus*), sometimes called grey mangrove, is also found in Costa Rica, and it too is a member of the Combretaceae family.

Red mangroves (named after the dark, red wood found under their bark) are the most saline-tolerant types of mangrove

ABOVE: *Red mangroves (Rhizophoraceae) absorb oxygen through their prop roots, which also give stability in strong winds and tides.*
OPPOSITE, ABOVE: *Wood Storks (*Mycteria americana*) are attracted to turtle-nesting beaches on the north Pacific coast.*
OPPOSITE, BELOW: *Black Vultures (*Coragyps atratus*) dry their wings in the morning sun on Ostional Beach.*

and grow on the water's edge, where the ground is submerged for most or all of the day. Black mangroves grow a little higher up the shore where the ground is only flooded at high tide. Tea and white mangroves and Buttonwood Trees are restricted to the very upper reaches of the intertidal zone and just beyond.

For several hours of every day, the intertidal zone is immersed in salty, brackish water that seeps into and saturates the mud in which the trees grow. In order to survive under these conditions, mangrove trees must cope with a water supply that is highly concentrated with salt, and a substrate that is waterlogged and hence highly deficient in oxygen.

To combat the high levels of salinity, both black and white mangrove trees take up the water from the ground, but then actively remove the salt through tiny glands on their leaves. Rainfall eventually washes the salt from the plant and it returns to the water. After several weeks of no rainfall during the dry season, these trees' leaves can be seen to be covered with salt crystals. Red mangroves remove excess salt by storing it in old leaves, which then take the salt with them when they fall off the plant. Most mangrove species also deal with the problem of the saline water at its source; they allow water to filter into their roots, but a lot of the salt molecules are kept out by special cell membranes. In this way red mangroves can reportedly remove up to 90 per cent of the salt from the water they use.

The roots of mangrove plants need oxygen to survive and they normally obtain it from the soil. This is because even though the plant's leaves take in oxygen, it would take too long to transport it down to the roots. The problem faced by mangrove trees is that the mud they grow in has very low levels of oxygen. To overcome this, they grow roots above the ground to obtain their oxygen directly from the air. Red mangroves have large prop roots that sprout from their trunks above the waterline and arch down into the water. In addition to providing the tree with stability in stormy weather, these structures are covered with pores through which oxygen is absorbed.

Black mangroves use the same technique to obtain oxygen, but their roots have an entirely different structure. The primary roots grow just below the surface of the mud, and from these a multitude of pencil-like peg roots extends 10 to 15 cm into the air, like snorkels. These roots are called pneumatophores, and they too have pores through which oxygen can pass. Tea mangrove trees have deeply fluted trunks formed from layers of thick adventitious roots that emerge from the trunk about 1 m above the ground. These roots have a soft, porous surface that permits the influx of oxygen. Because white mangroves and

ABOVE, LEFT: *The salt that black mangroves (Acanthaceae) take up from the substrate is excreted through their leaves.*
LEFT: *The mangrove fiddler crab (Uca sp.) is abundant in the black mangrove swamp of the Tamarindo Wildlife Refuge.*
OPPOSITE: *Black mangrove shrubs growing in the Tamarindo Wildlife Refuge.*

Buttonwood Trees live at the very top of the intertidal zone where flooding is infrequent, they can survive without aerial roots.

The tangled mass of aerial and underground roots that a mangrove produces has an additional function that benefits the mangrove ecosystem as a whole. They help to maintain the physical structure of the shoreline by trapping sediment and floating, organic debris that is carried in by the tide. This can help to significantly counteract the erosion caused by a storm or hurricane. In the long term, an ecological succession can occur, where the trapped sediment becomes new land that is eventually taken over by non-mangrove land plant species.

Trees that grow on land that is constantly flooded by salt water must produce seeds that can either quickly produce

ABOVE: *The Boa Constrictor (*Boa constrictor*) hunts iguanas, birds and medium-sized mammals in the trees of mangrove forests.*

roots and establish themselves on the mud below, or else survive what is sometimes many months afloat in the ocean. Many mangrove species are viviparous, which means the seeds begin to germinate before they drop off the plant. Both red and black mangroves reproduce in this way. The mother tree provides high levels of nutrients to fuel this development, which represents a heavy investment in each seed, and as a consequence fewer are produced than in most tree species.

THE FAUNA

A mangrove forest provides essential feeding, breeding and nursery grounds for an abundance of different organisms. This land of mud and murky waters is such a biologically diverse habitat because it is so nutrient-rich; from the trees falls a continuous flow of dead leaves, bark, flowers and seeds that are decomposed and fed upon by bacteria, fungi, algae and other micro-organisms. This rotting vegetation and its hosts are in turn fed on by worms, snails, prawns, small fish and crabs.

The calm, muddy waters of the canals and creeks that weave through the mangrove forest provide ideal nursery and feeding grounds for many fish, crustaceans, molluscs and the two largest reptiles in Costa Rica, the Spectacled Caiman and American Crocodile (*Crocodylus acutus*).

When the high tide recedes, exposing large areas of water-logged sludge, scores of fiddler crabs (*Uca* spp.) appear from their deep burrows to feed on micro-organisms in the mud. They often emerge in such high numbers that the ground can appear to be moving. The huge, brightly coloured claws of the male fiddler crabs are hard to miss against the dark brown colour of the mud. This cumbersome-looking appendage is waved in the air during courtship and territorial displays. Though a larger claw may intimidate more competing males and impress more females, it will also attract the attention of more predators. The Common Black Hawk (*Buteogallus anthracinus*) is a specialized crab-feeder commonly seen around mangroves. It attacks crabs on the ground by pouncing on them from the air or sometimes chasing them on foot. In defence, fiddler crabs react quickly to the slightest movement above them by scurrying back to their burrows. At night-time, other mangrove predators such as plovers and raccoons feed on fiddler crabs.

The canopy of the mangrove forest is rich in wildlife, especially birds. The Mangrove Hummingbird (*Amazilia boucardi*),

which is endemic to Costa Rica, snowy-white Yellow-billed Cotinga (*Carpodectes antoniae*) and bright yellow Mangrove Warbler (*Dendroica petechia erithachorides*) spend much of their time feeding among the mangrove vegetation. Ospreys, kingfishers and herons perch on branches overlooking the cloudy waters, watching for the ripples of swimming fish.

Every day at dusk the gentle quiet of the mangrove is interrupted by the arrival of flocks of squawking and honking birds that come to roost in the treetops. Brown Pelicans, Roseate Spoonbills, White Ibises, Green Ibises (*Mesembrinibis cayennensis*), Snowy Egrets, Boat-billed Herons (*Cochlearius cochlearius*), Green-backed Herons (*Butorides virescens*) and Scarlet Macaws all seek the safe sanctuary of mangrove trees in which to spend the night. Because the trees are surrounded by salty water or deep mud, they are effectively isolated from many land predators such as cats and large snakes.

These birds share the trees with a number of different animals. The Mangrove Tree Crab (*Aratus pisonii*) is found on almost every aerial root and trunk in the forest. It has sharp tips at the ends of its legs that allow the crab to climb effortlessly up the bark where it feeds on leaves, adult insects and larvae. When threatened, it will simply drop back into the safety of the water. Reptiles such as the Green Iguana, Black Spiny-tailed

ABOVE: *The rare Scarlet Macaw (*Ara macao) *is one of the many bird species that roost in Costa Rica's mangrove forests.*

Iguana and Boa Constrictor can be found in mangrove trees, and Crab-eating Raccoons (*Procyon cancrivorus*), White-nosed Coatis and White-faced Capuchins all forage the vegetation and ground for crabs and molluscs.

CONSERVATION

The creation of national parks and reserves has helped to protect significant areas of mangrove forest and coastline in Costa Rica. Nevertheless, their destruction continues outside of these regions. Land is cleared for the construction of hotels, golf courses, condominiums, shrimp farms and artificial ponds that are used for the commercial extraction of salt. Mangrove trees are cut down to provide timber and firewood, and chemical pesticides, fertilizers and sediment that run off deforested land upriver add to the devastation.

On the beaches, turtles are easily deterred from coming ashore to lay their eggs if confronted with noise or lights. Human development on wild areas adjacent to turtle-nesting beaches can seriously disturb a process that has been uninterrupted for millions of years.

CHAPTER 2
THE WILDLIFE OF COSTA RICA

In the mountains, lowlands and coastal areas of Costa Rica live about 5 per cent of all the world's recorded animal species. Intriguing mammals such as the Baird's Tapir, Two-toed Sloth and Kinkajou inhabit the forests, as well as the stealthy hunters, the Jaguar and Puma. Of the country's avian fauna, the Resplendent Quetzal, Scarlet Macaw and Keel-billed Toucan show off some of the brightest colours in the forests. The American Crocodile, Boa Constrictor and several poison dart frog species are just some of the many reptiles and amphibians that thrive in the tropical climate, along with more than a third of a million invertebrate species, including leaf-cutter ants, the Hercules Beetle and almost fifty species of tarantula.

LEFT: *A Chestnut-mandibled Toucan (*Ramphastos swainsonii*) manoeuvres down a tree branch to feed on clusters of hanging fruits.*

INVERTEBRATES

Costa Rica's tropical forests are home to millions upon millions of flying, hopping, crawling and wriggling invertebrates from an estimated 370,000 species. Approximately 95 per cent of the estimated number of these invertebrate species are insects, which in turn are believed to account for about 70 per cent of all species of living organism in the country. These figures remain estimates because of the vast number of species that have yet to be formally identified.

Visits to tropical forests in Costa Rica will reveal some of the countless invertebrates – animals without backbones including insects, spiders, scorpions, millipedes, mites, snails and worms among many others – living in this environment. Butterflies dance in the air, ants swarm across the forest floor, bright beetles crawl over decomposing logs and praying mantids lurk among the vegetation in ambush.

BUTTERFLIES AND MOTHS

Just over 1,500 butterfly species have been recorded in Costa Rica, and there are probably ten times this many moths. In comparison, there are only about 750 butterfly species in the United States and 56 resident species in the United Kingdom.

BELOW: *The metallic blue of a morpho butterfly (*Morpho *sp.) can startle an approaching predator when the butterfly takes flight.*

In Costa Rica butterflies and moths live in all natural habitats between the coasts and the cloud forests of the central mountain range. During the dry season, however, when food is much scarcer in the arid forests of the north-west, some populations migrate to nearby pockets of riparian forest or over the mountains to the more humid Atlantic slope. In the south Pacific lowlands, resident populations of the black and green Ducktail Butterfly (*Urania fulgens*) migrate to the Caribbean lowlands in search of food, though not always as a result of the climate. The caterpillars of these insects feed on a toxic liana of the genus *Omphalea*. This plant responds to being grazed on by producing more concentrated toxins, which the caterpillars are eventually unable to tolerate. After four to six years of feeding on these plants in one area, the population of butterflies migrates in huge numbers across the central *cordillera* in search of ungrazed *Omphalea*.

In most cases, however, butterflies and moths are beneficial to plants because they pollinate the flowers on which they feed. In this way they play a vital role in the survival of tropical ecosystems. Many animals are also reliant on the larva and adult form of these insects – a large number of bats and other mammals as well as birds depend on them as one of their main sources of food.

Of all the vibrantly coloured and ornately patterned butterflies and moths in Costa Rica, the morpho butterflies (*Morpho* spp.) are possibly the most striking. Resident in both rainforests and cloud forests on both slopes, the upper surfaces of these butterflies' wings are metallic blue – a relatively rare

colour in nature. Interestingly, this colour is not due to a pigment, as in most butterflies, but is a result of the physical structure of the wings themselves. The layered scales that cover the wings reflect blue light but effectively absorb the wavelengths of all other colours, meaning that the wings look blue. When a morpho lifts off from its perch to escape from a predator, the sudden flash of blue from its wings may momentarily startle the hunter and give the butterfly enough time to fly out of range.

The glasswing or clearwing butterflies, of the subfamily Ithomiinae, have almost no wing scales at all. Their transparent wings allow the colours of the surrounding vegetation to pass through them, providing a degree of camouflage from predators in the forest understory where they live. This camouflage is very useful when feeding for long periods of time, which these and other butterflies do at rotting fruits and bird droppings. The droppings provide the female butterflies with important nitrogen compounds, which they are believed to incorporate into their eggs. Butterflies in the forest are most easily approached and photographed when they are feeding in this way.

Some butterfly species in Costa Rica have patterns of bright colours on their wings to warn predators of their very unpleasant taste. Caterpillars of the Heliconiinae subfamily, such as the black and white Zebra Longwing (*Heliconius charitonius*) and the bright orange Julia Butterfly, feed on passion flower vines that contain mild toxins. These poisonous chemicals accumulate in the body of the caterpillar and remain there after its metamorphosis into an adult. It is these chemicals that give the adult its disagreeable taste.

Other caterpillars take their defence one step further and have rows of poisonous spines on their backs to deter predators. One such example is the larva of the Limacodid Moth (*Acharia nesea*) from the Caribbean lowlands. Its needle-sharp spines contain histamine that causes pain and swelling to skin if touched.

ABOVE: *A glasswing butterfly (Ithomiinae) feeds on rotting fruits in the rainforest.*
BELOW: *The stinging spines of the Limacodid Moth (*Acharia nesea*) larva are a convincing deterrent against would-be predators.*

BEETLES

The number of beetle species that live in Costa Rica is estimated at tens of thousands. A significant number have been identified and named, though the majority have yet to be officially recorded. Many feed on dead leaves, rotting wood, decomposing fruits, dead animals or even, in the case of the dung beetle *Dichotomius colonicus*, on animal faeces. In this way, they play an important role in 'cleaning' the environment in which they live.

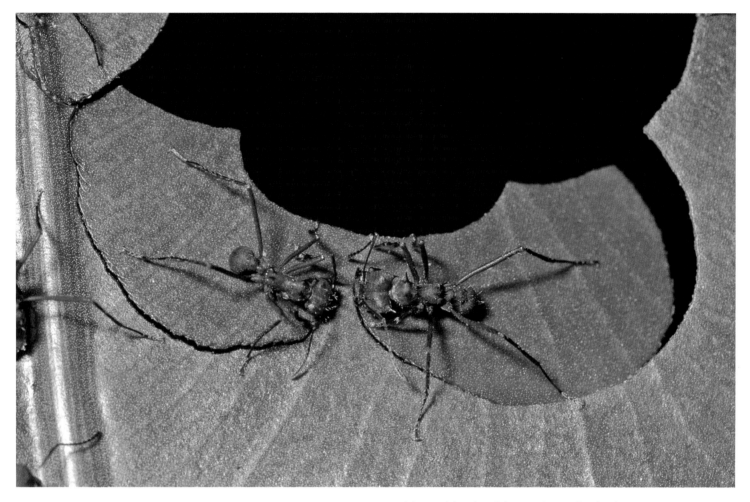

ABOVE: *Leaf-cutter ants cut out sections of a leaf with their huge, scissor-shaped jaws.*

Countless other species graze on living plants, insects and fungi. Two of the world's most beautiful beetles live in the highlands of Costa Rica. The golden beetles *Chrysina aurigans* and *Chrysina batesi* have metallic gold exoskeletons that shine brilliantly in the gloomy understory of the mist-covered cloud forest. There is also a variant of *Chrysina batesi* that is coloured metallic silver.

Equally eye-catching, the gigantic Elephant Beetle (*Megasoma elephas*) and Hercules Beetle live in dense pristine forests in Costa Rica, where they feed on fallen fruits and tree sap. Males of both species have elongated horns that they use in fighting other males when competing for a female or food. These horns can give adults a total length of 12 to 15 cm.

At the time when these beetles evolved their large horns, they also developed an incredible strength with which to wield them against their competitors. The Hercules Beetle in particular is so strong that it can move objects that are hundreds of times heavier than its own body. Such an accomplishment has led it to be labelled the strongest animal on Earth in proportion to its body weight.

Another giant beetle that inhabits the wildernesses of Costa Rica is the male Harlequin Beetle (*Acrocinus longimanus*). This resident of lowland forests has a body that grows to 7 cm in length and elongated front legs that can extend to twice that distance. These enormous appendages appear to aid the insect when it climbs. True to its name, the Harlequin Beetle has a variegated black, orange and yellow pattern on its wing cases, which may deter predators from attacking it.

ANTS

These are by far the most abundant insects in tropical forests. There is very little of the forest floor or vegetation that is not scoured by foraging worker ants as they search for food and materials to take back to their nests.

Leaf-cutter ants, of the genera *Atta* and *Acromyrmex*, are the most noticeable ants in Costa Rica. They form lengthy columns of workers that march along branches, down tree trunks and over the ground carrying fragments of brightly coloured leaves or flowers in their jaws. They carry this plant material back to their nest, where it is mashed up by other, smaller workers and used to cultivate a fungus in their multi-chambered, underground nest. This fungus grows swollen structures called gongylidia, which the ants then eat.

In the forest, the workers search from the forest floor to the canopy for suitable leaves and flowers that the fungus will grow on. The ants cut out a section of the leaf or flower with their jaws and then carry it back to the nest, which can some-

times be hundreds of metres away. The relationship between the leaf-cutter ants and the fungus is mutualistic, with both organisms depending on the other for their survival. The fungus is given a substrate on which to grow in safety, and competing fungi are removed by the ants. In return, the ant colony receives a constant and nutritious source of food for its millions of members.

Leaf-cutter ants are widespread in the rainforests and cloud forests of Costa Rica up to an altitude of about 2,000 m. They even nest in green areas of San José. Other ant species in Costa Rica are less peaceful than the leaf-cutters and forage for living organisms rather than plants. Army ants are as efficient at removing animals from an area of forest as leaf-cutter ants are at defoliating it. Of the approximately 150 species of army ant in the American tropics, *Eciton burchelli* has the largest and most destructive swarms. Once a day,

ABOVE: *Leaf-cutter ants carry leaf parts back to their nest, where they are used to cultivate a fungus upon which the colony feeds.* BELOW: *The enormous, 2.5 cm-long Bullet Ant (*Paraponera clavata*) stuns prey such as this grasshopper with a powerful bite or sting.*

their colonies send out hundreds of thousands of worker ants, each 1–1.5 cm long. They swarm over a chosen area of forest and kill all living creatures that remain in their path. This dark mass of ants climbs to the top of each tree and down again as the ants hunt invertebrates and even small vertebrates that are not fast or nimble enough to escape. When one file of ants reaches a small hole or gap in the vegetation the first worker will lie across it to form a bridge that the ants behind it can cross. Every time the ants encounter a prey animal they swarm around and kill it with bites and stings. The animal is then cut into pieces and left to be collected on the ants' return journey to their colony. At the end of their foraging expedition, which can last eight or nine hours, the ants return to their starting point with all of their food and form a temporary nest called a bivouac, usually in a hollow tree or log. This bivouac is created by layers of workers that cling together and surround the queen of the colony and her developing young. After a number of days the colony migrates to a new area, where it can find fresh prey.

The Bullet Ant (*Paraponera clavata*), which lives in the Caribbean rainforests of Costa Rica, is another highly aggres-

BELOW: *Leaf katydids (Pseudophyllinae) have evolved extraordinarily elaborate camouflage.*

sive ant species. This enormous, 2.5 cm-long insect is nicknamed 'the 24-hour Ant' in Spanish because that is about how long the pain from its sting takes to subside in humans. This sting is considered the most painful of all insect stings in the world.

Bullet Ants normally build their nests among the roots of a tree. The colony's workers forage predominantly in the canopy for drops of nectar-rich water and insects, which they carry back to their nest in their jaws. They attack insect prey with bites or a sting that paralyzes the victim's nervous system.

BEES AND WASPS

As is the case with ants, many species of bee and wasp in Costa Rica live in social groups. The stingless bee species *Trigona fulviventris* lives in colonies of several thousand individuals in dry forests and rainforests around the country. It builds its nest in the base of a tree, from which workers fly through the forest in search of nectar, pollen and nest-building materials such as plant resins, mud and fungi. Paper wasps of the genus *Polistes* are one of the most common wasp species in Costa Rica. These large, black and yellow wasps build unique nests that are characterized by their open-ended, hexagonal cells. They hang from vegetation or under the roofs of buildings.

Many bees play a very important role in their respective habitats by pollinating a wide selection of plants. Orchid bees of the *Euglossini* tribe visit a range of orchids to collect chemicals that are believed to help them attract females during courtship displays. When a bee lands on an orchid, some of the flower's pollen is deposited onto one specific area of the insect's body. The next time the bee lands on an orchid of the same species, which has an identical flower arrangement, the part of the bee that is covered in pollen comes into contact with the stigma of the new flower and the pollen is transferred, thus completing the pollination process. Orchids of other species have their stigmas in slightly different positions, so if the bee visits them the pollen is not transferred and wasted.

There are various wasps in Costa Rica that are parasites of ants, caterpillars or spiders. The Tarantula Hawk Wasp (*Pepsis formosa*) is a 5 cm-long wasp with a metallic, dark blue body and bright orange wings. It attacks tarantulas on the forest floor, a duel that usually involves a fierce struggle between these two aggressive predators. The wasp tries to paralyze the spider with its sting and if successful, it drags the tarantula across the ground and into either the tarantula's own burrow or into a hole the wasp has dug itself nearby. The wasp then lays an egg on top of the spider and leaves the burrow sealed. When the egg hatches, the wasp larva feeds on the paralyzed tarantula, which, because it is still alive, provides the larva with a fresh source of food during its development.

INSECT CAMOUFLAGE

One way for an animal to evade its predators is to simply hide. This can be done by remaining completely out of view, or by taking on the appearance of the surroundings. This latter characteristic has developed in some species through millions of years of evolution – and no group of animals has developed more diverse and complex systems of camouflage than the insects.

In the dry forests, rainforests and cloud forests of Costa Rica, a host of species has evolved body forms and textures that are so similar to the surroundings that the insects often still can't be seen even when they are pointed out. Many remain motionless during the day and only break their cover and begin moving when darkness falls.

The leaf katydids of the subfamily Pseudophyllinae have elaborate body designs and surface textures that mimic leaves. The species that live among dead leaves on the forest floor are usually brown or yellow, and those that remain among living

BELOW: *A Leaf-mimic Mantid (*Choeradodis rhombicollis) *devours a moth caught in midair with its long, barbed forelegs.*

ABOVE: *The synchronized mating calls of scores of male cicadas can drown the sounds of almost all the other animals in the forest.*

vegetation tend to be green. The Lichen Katydid (*Markia hystrix*) looks almost identical to the white lichen that it feeds on in its cloud forest habitat.

In the dry forests of north-west Costa Rica, the Guanacaste Stick Insect (*Calynda bicuspis*) looks just like another twig in the foliage when it folds its legs along the length of its body. This insect grows to as large as 12 cm long but is still almost invisible when resting in vegetation.

A number of moths from the family Geometridae have superbly camouflaged wings that match the tree trunk or leaf litter on which they rest. The caterpillars of the Citrus Swallowtail Butterfly (*Papilio thoas*) bear a very close resemblance to bird droppings, and the pupae and caterpillars of several butterfly and moth species such as the leaf moth *Oxytenis modestia* have false eye-spots that make them look like snakes.

Insects don't only use camouflage for the purpose of defence. Praying mantids, which belong to the family Mantidae, use a combination of camouflage and stealth in order to approach their prey without being noticed. In Costa Rica some mantids are green or a mottled greenish-brown to camouflage them among living vegetation or the trunks of trees. Others, which live among dead or sun-bleached leaves

and fallen branches on the forest floor, are brown or almost white. The Leaf-Mimic Mantid (*Choeradodis rhombicollis*) has even evolved an enlarged, hooded thorax that gives the insect the shape and colour of a green leaf. Mantids creep up on their prey with very slow movements. These expert hunters have long front legs lined with razor-sharp barbs. Once a mantid is close enough to its intended victim, it strikes out and snares the animal with these barbs. It is then eaten alive. Mantids sometimes ambush moths flying around a light bulb at night; their barbs are so sharp that they can catch one of these insects in mid-flight.

OTHER INSECTS

The forests of Costa Rica are home to many other groups of insect. Flies, dragonflies and damselflies that hunt other invertebrates in the air are found in most forested areas. The Helicopter Damselfly (*Megaloprepus coerulatus*) snatches spiders from leaves or even from the centre of their sticky web. It then lands and chews off the spider's head and legs before feeding on the succulent abdomen. This huge damselfly has a 10 cm-long abdomen and a wingspan of up to 18 cm – larger than that of any damselfly in the world. Despite its size, however, it still shows exceptional manoeuvrability when approaching prey. The flight of these insects is a wonder to watch. Their wings are a deep blue colour with a patch of white at each tip. When in motion, they produce a blur that is similar to that produced by the rotating blades of a helicopter.

Another winged hunter, the robber fly *Pilica formidolosa*, is adept at capturing flying insects in mid-air. This 3 cm-long member of the Asilidae family sits on a tree trunk or branch carefully watching other insects that fly past. Its large compound eyes provide it with excellent vision and when it spots a wasp, beetle or fly of a manageable size it takes off in pursuit. After catching it, the robber fly stabs the insect with its sharp proboscis and injects a powerful neurotoxin that causes immediate death. It additionally injects digestive enzymes that quickly dissolve the insect's internal organs, which the robber fly then feeds on.

Dozens of species of 'true bug' from the order Hemiptera thrive in Costa Rica, including cicadas, thorn bugs, shield bugs and aphids.

Cicadas are winged, beetle-like insects that are much better known for their calls than their appearance. Most of the 20 or more species found throughout Costa Rica are seldom seen because they live in the forest canopy, where they pierce the bark of trees to feed on the sap within. The mating call of male cicadas is one of the loudest created by any insect. The sound is similar to that of grasshoppers and often the calls of many individuals will rise and fall in synchrony, drowning out all other sounds in the forest.

Few insects have a body shape as bizarre as that of the thorn bugs of the Membracidae family. Their enlarged protho-

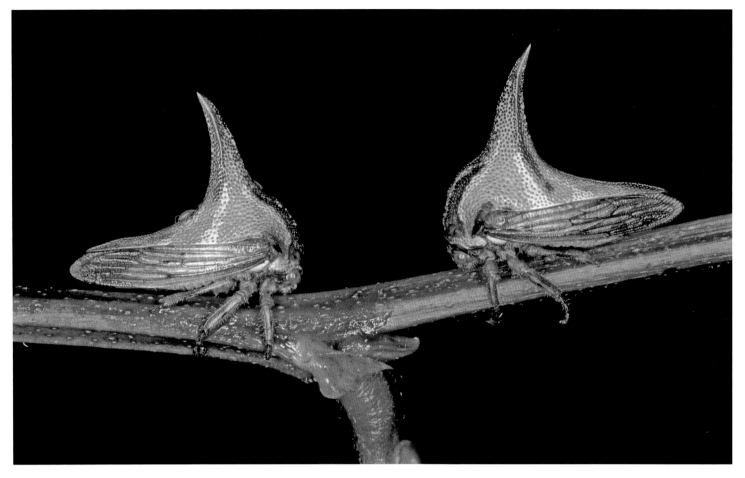

ABOVE: *The heavily armoured body of the thorn bug* Umbonia crassicornis *keeps it safe from most predators.*

rax makes their body closely resemble a sharp thorn, which helps to camouflage these insects from predators and also makes them look as unpalatable as possible if they are spotted. One of the most widespread species in Costa Rica is *Umbonia crassicornis*, which has an unexplained preference for disturbed areas of forest. Its colourful, 1 cm-long body is green with yellow stripes that lead up to the red tip of its 'thorn'. Typical of the order Hemiptera, this species and the other 30 or more species of thorn bug in Costa Rica have piercing and sucking mouthparts, which they use to extract the juices of their host plant.

SPIDERS AND OTHER INVERTEBRATES

Spiders in Costa Rica demonstrate a variety of impressive tactics to catch their prey. Many spin webs, others prepare ambushes on the forest floor and some simply chase down and leap on top of their victim.

The spiders that sit in the middle of a web they have spun across an open area between branches or stems in a tropical rainforest can potentially trap and quickly kill a multitude of flying insects. However, by sitting in the centre of such a web they make themselves very noticeable to predators and must therefore compensate either with camouflage or by appearing

unpalatable and dangerous. For example, several species of thorn spider have brightly coloured abdomens with protruding spines. It is likely that the combination of bright colour and a spiny abdomen deters many birds from feeding on them. The female Golden Orb Spider (*Nephila clavipes*) also spins its web out in the open and helps ward off predators with its very long yellow and black legs – a popular combination of warning colours in nature. This arachnid is the largest web-spinning spider in Costa Rica; adult females can have a leg span of 10 cm and they build webs up to 1 m or more wide. The male is many times smaller and can be easily identified by its bright red abdomen; it sits in the web close to the female.

This spider acquired its name from the deep yellow colour of its silk, which is the strongest tested material of its kind in nature. Large butterflies and wasps that blunder into its web find it extremely difficult to fight their way out, and even fast-flying hummingbirds are occasionally netted by the webs. Laboratory experiments have shown that its fibres are stronger and tougher than those of Kevlar, the material used in bullet-proof vests. Golden Orb Spider silk is also extremely elastic, and scientists have been investigating its usefulness in surgery, where it could be used to stitch wounds, create artificial tendons and help repair severed neurons.

Numerous species of spider in Costa Rica hunt their prey on foot. These spiders can sense the smallest of vibrations in the vegetation or the ground on which they are standing,

which alerts them to the approach of potential food. Wolf spiders and wandering spiders, of the families Lycosidae and Ctenidae, either sit and wait for prey to pass or actively search for it, typically at night. They usually eat insects, although large wandering spiders sometimes capture small lizards such as anoles.

The largest spiders that hunt on foot are the tarantulas, of which about fifty species exist in Costa Rica. Famous for their size, some species have leg spans of 15 cm when fully grown. Between them they inhabit both low- and mid-elevation forested areas throughout Costa Rica. During the day these giant arachnids rest in burrows in the ground, inside hollow trees or logs, or within funnels of silk-bound moss and dead leaves on tree trunks. During the night they hunt virtually any animal that is smaller in size than themselves, including both reptiles and mammals.

ABOVE: *This wandering spider (Cupiennius getazi) is large enough to feed on small lizards and frogs as well as invertebrates.*
OPPOSITE, ABOVE: *The Zebra Tarantula (Aphonopelma seemani) emerges from its underground tunnel at dusk to ambush prey.*
OPPOSITE, BELOW: *A jumping spider (Salticidae) overpowers a winged ant of its own size.*
BELOW: *The web fibres of the Golden Orb Spider (Nephila clavipes) are so strong that they can even trap a small hummingbird.*

The Zebra Tarantula is common in grassy clearings in the dry north-west of Costa Rica. It spends the daylight hours in its burrow about 10 cm below the ground. At dusk it climbs to the entrance of the burrow and waits for a suitably sized insect to walk past. The tarantula can detect the ground vibrations of even a small insect as it walks. Once the prey is in range, the spider lunges at it and drags it back into its burrow in the blink of an eye. The tarantula kills the animal by injecting it with venom through its fangs. It then sprays digestive fluids over its victim and sucks up the resulting meal through its tiny mouth.

In the mid-elevation rainforests and cloud forests of the country, the Costa Rican Redleg Tarantula (*Megaphobema mesomelas*) also spends the day in a burrow that it or another animal has dug. Unlike the Zebra Tarantula, however, this species roams across the forest floor in search of its prey.

Possibly the most impressive hunting technique of all the spiders in Costa Rica is that of the jumping spiders found throughout the country. These small arachnids of the Salticidae family only grow to between 1 and 1.5 cm in length but are capable of making jumps many times that distance when hunting. Jumping spiders have excellent vision and normally feed during the day. Their prey is often as large as they are but the spider gains the element of surprise with its jump and quickly immobilizes a victim with its strong legs and potent venom.

Also in the tropical forests of Costa Rica, hordes of scorpions, millipedes and centipedes creep through leaf litter and decomposing logs, freshwater shrimps and crabs lurk at the bottoms of streams and an incalculable number of other invertebrates such as snails and worms play their roles in one of the most biologically rich lands on the planet.

AMPHIBIANS

The rainforests and cloud forests of Costa Rica receive between 2 and 7 m of rainfall per year. These huge quantities of water feed countless streams, form a myriad of temporary and permanent ponds, and create innumerable cool and damp hiding places in the vegetation and on the forest floor where amphibians can rest, feed and reproduce.

In Costa Rica the class Amphibia is represented by 133 species of frog and toad, 43 species of salamander and 4 species of the worm-like caecilians. Approximately 20 per cent of these species are endemic. The majority inhabit humid, lowland rainforest though there are a number of species that live in dry forest, cloud forest or around human settlements and agricultural land.

Frogs and toads (the distinction between the two is arbitrary) are the most noticeable amphibians in Costa Rica, especially during the wetter months of May to November, when their noisy mating and territorial calls reverberate through the forests at night. These singing amphibians are easy to locate in the darkness with a torch, the light of which is strongly reflected by the animals' retinas. The lizard-like salamanders are rarely seen in Costa Rica because they are uncommon and remain hidden in the leaf litter or among dense vegetation. The species that live in Costa Rica do not congregate around water to mate as do frogs and toads. Instead, their eggs develop into adults on land.

The limbless caecilians are even more difficult to spot because they spend most of their lives burrowing under the ground in the rainforest. These worm-like amphibians push themselves through the soil in search of the insects and worms that they feed on. Their eyesight is almost non-existent; instead they rely on tiny chemosensory tentacles on their heads to detect their prey.

Amphibians absorb a significant proportion of the oxygen they require through their thin skin (even though many have a functioning pair of lungs). To achieve this, the skin must be

BELOW: *The Red-eyed Tree Frog (*Agalychnis callidryas*) is one of the most vibrantly coloured animals in Costa Rica.*

kept moist, which is why most amphibians inhabit humid environments and avoid the dehydrating effect of the sun's rays by being active at night or staying in the shadows during the day. The skin of amphibians is also one of their best defences. It produces a toxin that kills fungi and bacteria that would otherwise colonize its moist surface. This also makes the animal distasteful to potential predators. In most species this toxin is mild, though toads from the genus *Bufo* and the poison dart frogs produce a much more potent secretion, which can be harmful even to large mammals.

TREE FROGS

The forty-three species of the tree frog family Hylidae that inhabit Costa Rica spend most of their lives in trees, though they do typically have an aquatic stage to their life cycles that brings them down to the forest floor. Consequently, tree frogs are usually only seen during their mating seasons, which coincide with the rainy months of the year.

Tree frogs are naturally very good climbers. They have a sucker pad on each of their fingers and toes; these pads allow them to scale vertical tree trunks and even sleep on the underside of a leaf. A number of species are very brightly coloured, while others have a skin colour that camouflages them well among vegetation. There are some that can change the tone or even the colour of their skin to match the branch or leaf they are resting on.

By far the most famous member of the Hylidae family in Costa Rica is the Red-eyed Tree Frog. This species has large red eyes, a bright green body, orange feet and blue and yellow striped flanks, which make it one of the most spectacularly coloured amphibians in the world. During the day, however, its skin is dark green or turquoise, which make the frog less visible to bird and snake predators. A resident of the Caribbean and south Pacific lowland rainforests, this 6 cm-long frog spends most of the year in the treetops, where it is active at night and feeds on insects. During the rainy season, it descends to the vegetation around areas of flooded ground or permanent ponds, where it searches for a mate. Females are attracted by the calls of males and after mating, they lay their eggs in a sticky gel on the undersides of leaves that overhang a still body of water. The gel keeps the eggs hydrated and provides some protection from predators. When the eggs hatch between seven and ten days later, the tadpoles wriggle out of the gelatinous coating and drop into the water below, where they develop into adults. Temporary, flooded pools on the forest floor are often chosen by the Red-eyed Tree Frog because they have no or very few fish, which will eat the tadpoles.

The Parachuting Red-eyed Tree Frog (*Agalychnis saltator*) from the Caribbean slope of Costa Rica is physically very similar to the Red-eyed Tree Frog in size and colour. It too descends from the canopy in the rainy season and does so in a most dramatic way. By using its spread-out feet as tiny para-

ABOVE: *The Masked Tree Frog (*Smilisca phaeota*) descends from the tree canopy during the rainy season to lay its eggs in puddles.*

chutes, this frog is able to leap from high up in the trees down to the vegetation on the forest floor without injury. Travelling in this manner makes it unlikely that the frog will meet predators on its journey down. Female Parachuting Red-eyed Tree Frogs congregate to lay their gel-covered eggs together on vines that hang above pools of water. Their tadpoles fall into the pool after they hatch, in the same manner that Red-eyed Tree Frog tadpoles do.

Instead of laying their eggs inside a waterproof gel to prevent them from drying out, some species of tree frog in Costa Rica lay their eggs on the surface of water. The Loquacious Tree Frog (*Hyla loquax*) is a muddy brown-coloured frog that descends from rainforest trees in the Caribbean lowlands to deposit its batch of eggs on large pools of still water. The Masked Tree Frog (*Smilisca phaeota*) does the same, although it chooses small puddles in which to leave its eggs. Its tadpoles hatch and metamorphose into adults in about one month – much faster than the tadpoles of most other tree frogs. This is because they face the danger of their puddle drying up during a prolonged dry spell. The Masked Tree Frog inhabits both Caribbean and Pacific rainforests in Costa Rica and is one of the tree frog species that can change the colour of its skin.

During the day it is normally tan with dark brown patches, which camouflages it exceptionally well when it is sleeping on a tree trunk or branch. At night, when the frog is active, this colour sometimes changes to green.

Another species that lays its eggs on the surfaces of rainforest ponds is the Milk Frog (*Phrynohyas venulosa*). This species from the Pacific lowlands is Costa Rica's largest frog, growing up to 11 cm in length. Remarkably, it can produce enough eggs in a single batch to cover over 1 sq m of water. It gets its name from the toxic white liquid that it secretes from its skin when it is attacked by a predator.

In the cloud forests and mountainous rainforests of Costa Rica, the Red-eyed Stream Frog (*Duellmanohyla uranochroa*) lays its eggs around running water as opposed to a pool. It attaches them to rocks or vegetation in the middle of a stream, where they are well protected from many terrestrial predators.

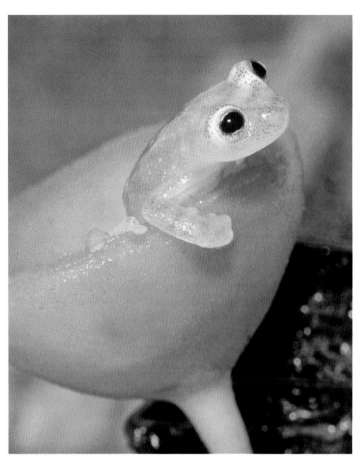

ABOVE: *The skin of the Reticulated Glass Frog (*Hyalinobatrachium valerioi*) is almost transparent.*

One species of tree frog in Costa Rica has a remarkable method of caring for its unborn offspring. After mating, the female Horned Marsupial Tree Frog (*Gastrotheca cornuta*) carries her large, fertilized eggs in a brood pouch on her back. The eggs measure 10–12 mm in diameter, making them the largest of all amphibians' eggs. The eggs stay with the female until they hatch weeks later as fully developed baby frogs. The Horned Marsupial Tree Frog is rare in Costa Rica; its known range is limited to areas of rainforest in the Caribbean lowlands south of the city of Limón.

GLASS FROGS

These are truly bizarre animals. When viewed from above they have a similar body shape to that of tree frogs of the Hylidae family, though glass frogs can be distinguished by their small size (with a maximum length of 2–3 cm) and the position of their eyes; glass frogs have forward-facing eyeballs and in tree frogs the eyes grow on either side of the head, facing sideways. When a glass frog is viewed from below, however, it looks like no other land animal in Costa Rica. The skin is partially, or in the case of the genus *Hyalinobatrachium*, almost totally trans-

parent. In the case of the latter, the animal's intestines, blood vessels, bones and sometimes even its beating heart are visible through the skin. This unique trait allows some light to pass through the frog from below, therefore giving the animal a very similar colour to that of the leaf or branch it is sitting on. Such camouflage makes it very difficult for predators to spot the frog during the day.

There are thirteen glass frog species in Costa Rica, all of which are arboreal and nocturnal. Two of the most common are Fleischmann's Glass Frog (*Hyalinobatrachium fleischmanni*) and the Emerald Glass Frog (*Centrolenella prosoblepon*). Both these species live in rainforests and cloud forests around the country and, like the other eleven species in Costa Rica, they migrate to vegetation close to streams during their mating season. All glass frog females lay their eggs on leaves that hang over the water and in many species one of the parents remains to guard them throughout the period of their development. The Reticulated Glass Frog (*Hyalinobatrachium valerioi*) is one species that demonstrates a very high level of parental care. The male has a spotted skin pattern that is almost identical to the cluster of eggs that it guards. This draws insects that eat or parasitize its eggs towards the frog and away from the real eggs – the frog then eats most of these insects.

POISON DART FROGS

The layers of dead leaves and rotting logs on the floor of Costa Rica's rainforests are home to a unique group of amphibian: the poison dart frogs. These frogs, of the family Dendrobatidae, are vibrantly coloured and grow to just 2–4 cm in length. They are active during the day and spend most of their time on the ground. In Costa Rica, they live in low- and mid-elevation rainforests on the Caribbean and Pacific slopes. Further afield, there are species that inhabit tropical forests from Nicaragua to Brazil. The best known, the Golden Poison Dart Frog (*Phyllobates terribilis*) from Colombia, is used by native Indians in the Amazon rainforest to provide poison for the tips of their hunting darts. This is one of the most poisonous creatures on

Earth – its poison is lethal to wild animals and humans alike. The poison dart frogs in Costa Rica also secrete neurotoxins through their skin, though none is as potent as that of the Golden Poison Dart Frog. The toxin of these frogs is derived from the chemical defences of the ants and termites that they eat. Consequently, poison dart frogs that are kept and fed in captivity gradually lose their ability to produce their skin toxin.

The easiest poison dart frog to find in Costa Rica is the Strawberry Poison Dart Frog (*Dendrobates pumilio*). It is common in the Caribbean lowlands and abundant in places such as La Selva Biological Station in Sarapiquí. This species typically has a red or orange body and dark blue legs, although some individuals are almost entirely red or orange. Like other poison dart frogs they are most active in the morning after a rain shower, when they walk and hop across the ground catching tiny insects with their sticky tongues. They avoid direct sunlight to prevent becoming dehydrated, and as the forest floor dries out on a sunny day, they retreat to the cool and damp spaces under the fallen vegetation.

The reproductive cycle of the Strawberry Poison Dart Frog is a fascinating display of parental care. The female lays her fertilized eggs under leaves on the forest floor and the male is left to guard them. From time to time he may urinate on the clutch to stop it from drying out. The female returns to sit with the eggs about a week later when they are ready to hatch. As each tadpole emerges, it wriggles onto her back and she carries it up into the vegetation, where she drops it into a tiny pool of standing water inside a plant such as a bromeliad. The female often leaves her offspring in different pools of water. During the development of her tadpoles, she periodically returns to each pool to deposit several of her nutrient-rich unfertilized eggs into the water; these are an important source of food for her offspring.

Other species of poison dart frog in Costa Rica care for their offspring in the same or a similar way. In the area of the Osa Peninsula, the female Granular Poison Dart Frog (*Dendrobates granuliferus*) transports and feeds her tadpoles just as the Strawberry Poison Dart Frog does. Also in the south-west of Costa Rica, the male Golfo Dulce Poison Dart Frog (*Phyllobates vittatus*) carries several of his tadpoles at a time as he climbs in search of suitable pools in which to leave them.

The Black and Green Poison Dart Frog (*Dendrobates auratus*) and the Lovely Poison Dart Frog (*Phyllobates lugubris*) from the Caribbean-side lowlands also carry their newly emerged tadpoles to temporary pools of water, where they feed on plants and tiny invertebrates. The combination of bright and dark colours that poison dart frogs display on their skin makes

ABOVE: *The Strawberry Poison Dart Frog (*Dendrobates pumilio*) is common in lowland rainforest of the Caribbean slope of Costa Rica.* BELOW: *The Black and Green Poison Dart Frog (*Dendrobates auratus*) is the largest of the toxic poison dart frogs in Costa Rica.*

ABOVE: *The endemic Golden Toad (*Bufo periglenes*) suddenly and mysteriously vanished from Costa Rica in 1989.*

them easy to spot against the browns and greens of the rainforest floor. Rather than attract predators, however, these colours send a clear warning to larger animals of the frogs' toxicity. Adult poison dart frogs therefore have very few predators. In Costa Rica, the Central American Bullfrog (*Leptodactylus pentadactylus*) and the Fire-bellied Snake (*Liophis epinephelus*) are known to feed on poison dart frogs. These predators are clearly immune to the paralyzing effects of the frogs' toxin though it is unclear exactly why.

OTHER AMPHIBIANS
Scores of other frog species from a number of different families live in Costa Rica. They include almost fifty species from the Leptodactylidae family, which includes the well-camouflaged small rain frogs of the genus *Eleutherodactylus*. Many of these frogs inhabit the leaf litter on the forest floor, where the mottled brown or tan colour of their skin makes them almost impossible to distinguish from the dead leaves. This camouflage allows them to be active during the day with little chance of being seen by predators.

Several frogs of the family Ranidae, which are commonly known as true frogs, live in a range of different habitats in Costa Rica. Forrer's Leopard Frog (*Rana forreri*) is one of the few amphibians in Costa Rica that lives in the hot, dry climate of the north-west, which represents the southern end of its geographical range. In sharp contrast, another member of the family, the Green–eyed Frog (*Rana vibicaria*), inhabits the cool cloud forests of the Talamanca mountain range.

The curiously egg-shaped Sheep Frog (*Hypopachus variolosus*) is one of the three species of the Microhylidae family found in Costa Rica. It sleeps during the day buried under the earth in dry forests and rainforests in the northern part of the country. At night it emerges to feed on insects on the ground.

The toad family, Bufonidae, is represented in Costa Rica by a number of species. The Cane Toad is the largest toad and amphibian in Costa Rica. Many adults grow to over 15 cm in length and can weigh more than 1 kg. These enormous terrestrial toads feed mostly on insects, spiders and frogs, but will sometimes eat a small mammal. Cane Toads produce a very toxic skin secretion, which means they are subject to very little predation and now live in many different habitats throughout Costa Rica. Only a small number of snakes such as the False Fer-de-Lance (*Xenodon rabdocephalus*) seem to be immune to the toad's toxin.

About half the size of the Cane Toad, the Green Climbing Toad (*Bufo coniferus*) is nimble enough to scale trees in search of its food. Such behaviour is rare among toads.

CONSERVATION
Populations of many toad and frog species in Costa Rica have mysteriously declined or disappeared since the late 1980s. The Golden Toad (*Bufo periglenes*), which was endemic to the Monteverde Cloud Forest Preserve, was estimated to have a population of about 1,500 individuals in 1987, but only one was sighted in 1988, and by 1989 it had completely vanished and hasn't been seen since. The Chiriquí Harlequin Frog (*Atelopus chiriquiensis*) and the Pico Blanco Toad (*Bufo fastidiosus*) from the Talamanca mountains and Holdridge's Toad (*Bufo holdridgei*) from the slopes of Barva Volcano have also not been seen for several years in Costa Rica. The Variable Harlequin Frog (*Atelopus varius*) now only exists in a very small, isolated population on the central Pacific coast.

Climate change, manmade pollution, a pathogenic fungus or perhaps a combination of these factors are considered the most likely explanations for the demise of these members of the Bufonidae family.

REPTILES

Reptiles fascinate us in a way that 'cute' or approachable mammals and birds do not. This might be because they provide us with a glimpse of what the long-extinct dinosaurs were really like, or maybe it is our enthralment with dangerous animals that creates the interest we have in reptiles such as the Neotropical Rattlesnake or the enormous American Crocodile. Whatever the reason may be, there are few places better on Earth to fuel this fascination than Costa Rica.

Cold-blooded animals thrive in hot climates. In Costa Rica the tropical temperatures, the variety of different habitats and the existence of both Atlantic and Pacific coastlines provide ideal natural environments for the 221 reptile species that have been recorded in the country; no doubt a number of others have yet to be discovered. Crocodiles and caimans lurk in bodies of fresh and brackish water throughout the lowlands of Costa Rica. Lizards and snakes abound in low-altitude rainforest, a surprising number inhabit the cooler climate of cloud forests and some lizards are even found above the tree-line on the *paramo* of the Talamanca mountain range. In addition, sea tur-tles nest on beaches along both coasts, while freshwater turtles live in and around a maze of inland waterways.

CROCODILES AND CAIMANS
In the cloudy waters of Costa Rica's mangrove swamps, estu-aries, lowland rivers and lagoons lives a truly giant reptile. The American Crocodile grows to over 4 m long and can weigh 700 kg, making it the largest reptile species in Central America.

BELOW: *An American Crocodile* (Crocodylus acutus) *in Tortuguero National Park gapes to cool its body temperature.*

In Costa Rica, American Crocodiles are most easily seen when basking on the mud banks of rivers and canals. They are common in the waterways leading to and inside Tortuguero National Park, and gather in unusually large numbers beneath the road bridge that spans the River Tárcoles next to Carara National Park on the central Pacific coast. Crocodiles are difficult to spot when they are in the water because even if they are on the surface, they keep their body submerged with only the eyes and snout visible. This is how they approach and surprise their larger prey such as otters, raccoons and aquatic birds; they keep this profile while slowly gliding to within striking distance, then lunge at the animal and trap it in their huge jaws. Most of the animals that crocodiles feed on are much smaller, however, such as fish, crabs and freshwater turtles.

Crocodiles sunbathe on sunny days to keep their body temperature at its optimum of about 30°C. When an animal begins to overheat, it opens its mouth in an act known as gaping. This allows the breeze to cool the crocodile's blood as it circulates through its mouth, and the animal's body temperature drops. If the crocodile is not able to cool down sufficiently by gaping it will slip from the river bank into the water.

Due to its size, the American Crocodile has no natural predators, though it is still hunted by humans for its skin. For this reason this species is much less common outside national parks and reserves than it is within them.

The Spectacled Caiman is a smaller relative of the American Crocodile and belongs to the alligator family Alligatoridae. It inhabits rivers, canals and lagoons in many areas of Costa Rica and, because of its smaller size, it ventures into narrower waterways and smaller bodies of water than the larger American Crocodile. It is not uncommon for several Spectacled Caimans to share a small, isolated pond formed when freshwater marshlands recede during the dry season.

The two species are physically very similar. The caiman can be identified, however, by the bony ridge between its eyes, which gives it its English name. In turn, the American

Crocodile can be distinguished by having a narrower head and mouth than the caiman.

Spectacled Caimans grow to a maximum length of about 2.5 m and their diet consists mainly of fish, frogs and waterbirds. Young caimans feed on snails and insects in the shallows, where their mottled skin colour camouflages them among the dead leaves and hides them from predators such as birds of prey and large herons.

IGUANAS

Large, four-legged reptiles also inhabit the land in Costa Rica. The Green Iguana is the largest, with some adults reaching a length of 2 m when fully grown. This lizard is identified by the drooped spines along its back, which are orange in males during the mating season, and a huge, round scale below each ear. When young, Green Iguanas are indeed bright green, but as they mature their skin becomes grey. Their long, clawed toes allow them to easily climb high into the forest canopy, often

ABOVE: *Young Green Iguanas (*Iguana iguana*) are much more striking than the mature, grey-coloured adults.*
ABOVE, LEFT: *The Spectacled Caiman (*Caiman crocodilus*) inhabits rivers and lagoons, feeding on fish, amphibians and wading birds.*

scaling vertical trunks and branches, where they feed on leaves and fruits. The top of a tree is also the perfect place to sunbathe; the Green Iguana requires a lot of heat from the sun to not only maintain its body temperature but also to stimulate cellulose-digesting bacteria in its stomach. The iguana relies on these micro-organisms to be able to digest the large amount of plant material it consumes every day.

The Green Iguana is one of the preferred foods of Jaguars, Pumas and Ocelots (*Leopardus pardalis*). The top of a tree is therefore a safe place for the iguana to forage and warm itself. Even though all three predators are able to climb into trees, the iguana is relatively safe at the end of a thin branch that can't support the weight of these hunters. Green Iguanas often climb

ABOVE: *The male Emerald Basilisk (*Basiliscus plumifrons*) uses its large crest to attract females during mating rituals.*

into trees that overhang a river or creek. If the reptile does find itself cornered by a cat or is buzzed by a large bird of prey, it can launch itself from its perch and plunge into the water below in order to escape, using its large tail to swim safely to land away from the predator.

Two other species from the Iguanidae family live in Costa Rica. By far the most common is the Black Spiny-tailed Iguana of the Pacific lowlands. This grey and black lizard lives in a hollow tree or a burrow in the earth. It feeds on fallen fruits on the ground, climbs trees to eat leaves and will also attack crabs, rodents and birds when the opportunity arises.

These iguanas are very common around ranger stations in national parks and reserves, where mature males can be observed bobbing their heads at each other to advertise their territorial claim to a patch of earth.

The third species of iguana found in Costa Rica is the Five-keeled Spiny-tailed Iguana (*Ctenosaura quinquecarinata*). This 50 cm-long dark green lizard is biologically very similar to the Black Spiny-tailed Iguana but it is rarely seen because it only lives in the dry forest of Santa Rosa National Park in the extreme north-west of the country.

BASILISKS

Basilisks are medium-sized lizards that live in forested areas bordering rivers, canals and lagoons. They have an ability that is unique among reptiles and indeed all vertebrates except for some waterbirds. When they are threatened by a predator or startled by a human, they flee by literally running across the surface of water on their hind legs. This behaviour has earned them the common name of 'Jesus Christ Lizard'.

To enable it to achieve this impressive feat, each toe on the hind feet of a basilisk is surrounded by a flap of skin, which effectively increases the surface area of the toe and the uplift it provides when the foot is pushed down. By moving their legs extremely quickly, these lizards are able to run for several metres without sinking. The younger and lighter the lizard is, the further it can run. If the basilisk hasn't reached land by the time it begins to sink it is fully capable of swimming the remaining distance. Basilisks also run on their hind legs when escaping from predators on land.

Branches, logs and boulders along the water's edge are the favourite perching spots of basilisks. From here they carefully study their surroundings for the movements of insects and spiders, their main sources of food.

Three species of basilisk live in Costa Rica. The bright green Emerald Basilisk (*Basiliscus plumifrons*) is the best known because of its colourful skin and the sail-like crests that males have running from their head to their tail. A resident species of the Caribbean slope, this lizard ventures further into the forest and away from water than the other basilisks. The Striped Basilisk (*Basiliscus vittatus*) also lives exclusively in the Caribbean lowlands and, as in the case of the Emerald Basilisk, the male has a bony crest on its head and smaller crests on its back and tail. However, the two species are easily distinguished by their colour. The Striped Basilisk is brown with two white lines that run down its back, which is very different from the vivid green of the Emerald Basilisk.

The lowlands of the Pacific coast are inhabited by the Common Basilisk (*Basiliscus basiliscus*), which is almost identical to the Striped Basilisk. The easiest way to tell them apart is to remember which coastline you are on!

ANOLES, WHIP-TAILED LIZARDS AND GECKOS

Small lizards are very common on the forest floor and in the undergrowth throughout Costa Rica. If one walks briskly along a jungle trail, a variety of these reptiles is likely to reveal itself by noisily scampering away from the intrusion across the leaf litter.

Anoles are the most commonly encountered lizards in many wild areas of Costa Rica. Their skin is a camouflaged mottled brown or green, and the different species range in body length between 4 and 12 cm, plus the tail.

The most remarkable feature of the anoles is the extendable flap of coloured skin, called a dewlap, which grows on the throat of the male. During mating behaviour and territorial displays, a muscle-controlled cartilage rod stretches the dewlap outwards into a fan shape. This display is usually accompanied by a bobbing of the head, and these two actions clearly announce the male's presence to competing males and potential female mates.

The dewlap of each anole species is different in colour and design and this is the method by which individual males can be most easily identified. The location of each anole can also help to determine its species. The terrestrial

Ground Anole (*Norops humilis*) lives in humid, low- and mid-elevation forests and has a bright orange dewlap with a yellow rim. The Indigo-throated Anole (*Norops sericeus*) has a yellow dewlap with a blue spot and is most common in the dry forests of Guanacaste. The tree-dwelling Canopy Anole (*Norops lemurinus*) has a small, dark red dewlap.

BELOW: *Like all Costa Rican basilisks, the Common Basilisk* (Basiliscus basiliscus) *can run for several metres across water.*

ABOVE: *A Ground Anole (*Norops humilis*) displays its brightly coloured dewlap during a territorial display.*

Anoles feed on insects and small spiders and are themselves hunted by a wide variety of snakes, birds and mammals. Their ability to camouflage themselves in the forest is therefore essential to their survival; the first defensive action of an anole is to lie flat and position itself on the opposite side of a branch or trunk to its predator. A game of hide-and-seek will ensue if the predator approaches, with the anole slowly creeping round the bark in an attempt to remain out of the sight of the larger animal. If, however, a predator gets too close to the lizard it will try and run away.

On sunny days in Costa Rica's lowland forests, another group of lizards is very active on the ground. The whip-tailed lizards are of a similar size to the anoles and are characterized by their very long tails, which can grow to twice the length of the rest of their bodies. These reptiles enjoy high temperatures and are among the few animals that will tolerate the burning temperatures of the sand on a tropical beach during the middle of the day. They forage for small invertebrates on the ground with jerky movements of their head and body and, when threatened by a predator, are capable of disappearing into the leaf litter with astonishing speed.

The most visually striking of the six whip-tail species in Costa Rica is the Deppe's Whip-tailed Lizard. Juveniles of this species have electric blue tails and bright yellow stripes on their abdomens. It is commonly encountered on beaches, sand dunes and in the adjacent vegetation.

Once the day begins to fade into night, the whiptails and most other lizards settle down to sleep. A small number of lizards, however, become active as darkness falls.

Several species of nocturnal gecko inhabit Costa Rica. These bulbous-eyed lizards from the Gekkonidae family prey on the multitude of insects and spiders that also become active at night. Most visitors to Costa Rica will hear the surprisingly loud, chirping call of the House Gecko (*Hemidactylus frenatus*) in or around their hotel at night. This species is found worldwide and only quite recently was it first recorded in Costa Rica, probably reaching the country on transport ships. It is easy to find around outdoor light bulbs after dark, where it snaps at flying insects that are attracted to the light. It also

feeds on insects inside buildings, and is able to scale smooth, painted walls and walk upside down across a ceiling.

Few animals can rival the climbing abilities of arboreal geckos. Their secret of defying gravity lies in their feet. On the underside of each toe, these lizards have hundreds of thousands of tiny bristles that interact to provide sufficient cohesion to support the animal's body weight even when running.

The Turniptail Gecko (*Thecadactylus rapicauda*) is another nocturnal species that is an expert climber. It is the largest gecko in Costa Rica, averaging around 15 cm in length, though it is rarely seen because it has a very cryptic, black and brown skin pattern and spends most of its time in trees.

SNAKES

The tropical forests of Costa Rica provide a wealth of ideal habitats for snakes. A total of 133 species has been recorded in the country, of which nineteen are highly venomous. They live in the rainforests, dry forests, cloud forests, mangroves, freshwater marshes and even in the ocean. Snakes are highly successful hunters that have changed very little since they evolved from their lizard-like ancestors tens of millions of years ago.

ABOVE: *The slim head of the Brown Vine Snake (*Oxybelis aeneus*) allows it to move stealthily in forest vegetation in search of food.*

The different snake species in Costa Rica vary greatly in behaviour and appearance. The Neotropical Slender Blindsnake (*Leptotyphlops goudotti*), for example, is just 20 cm long and feeds on nothing larger than an ant. At the other end of the scale, the Central American Bushmaster (*Lachesis stenophrys*) is the world's second largest poisonous snake, which may exceed 3 m in length and can swallow a rabbit whole.

Non-venomous Snakes

The majority of snakes are armed with some kind of venom that they use to overcome their prey. However, in many cases these chemicals are not actively injected into the animal through large fangs.

Some snakes have saliva that contains anti-coagulants, while others have small fangs at the backs of their mouths that drip a mild venom into their prey while they hold it in their jaws. These species are classed as non-venomous because they pose no serious threat to healthy humans. Most snake species in Costa Rica fall into this category, and are members of the Colubridae family.

Vine snakes are among the most common non-venomous snakes in Costa Rica. They have slender bodies and long, pointed heads that allow them to pass through very dense and tangled vegetation with ease. Fully grown adults grow to a length of 1–1.5 m and feed on lizards (especially anoles), mice, shrews, frogs and even some small birds.

The Brown Vine Snake (*Oxybelis aeneus*) and the green and yellow-coloured Short-nosed Vine Snake (*Oxybelis brevirostris*) follow their prey through bushes and small trees in the rainforest understorey and sometimes along the ground. Their colours and thin, vine-like bodies make them extremely difficult to distinguish from the surrounding vegetation. Most prey will feel the snake's bite before it realizes it is being stalked.

While photographing in the rainforest, I once saw a Brown Vine Snake snatch and swallow a pair of anole lizards that were mating on a branch. After the snake had made the initial strike, four legs and two tails were left protruding from its stretched mouth.

Once the Brown Vine Snake has its prey in its mouth, it injects a mild venom that immobilizes the struggling animal so that it can swallow it more easily. The Green Vine Snake (*Oxybelis fulgidus*) kills in this very same manner, but instead of following its prey, it ambushes it. The snake lies motionless, draped across the branches of a bush or tree, until an unsuspecting animal walks past. It then strikes as soon as the animal comes within range.

BELOW: *The Eyelash Viper (*Bothriechis schlegelii*) locates prey partly by 'smelling' the air with its tongue.*

Several other snake species weave their way through Costa Rica's rainforest vegetation in search of their own specific choice of prey. The diurnal Lower Montane Green Racer (*Drymobius melanotropis*) and the nocturnal Western Tree Snake (*Imantodes inornatus*) both feed predominantly on amphibians, the 2 m-long Bird-eating Snake (*Pseustes poecilonotus*) preys on birds and their eggs, and the Lichen-coloured Snail-eater (*Sibon longifrenis*) is highly adept at extracting snails from their shells before it eats them.

The largest snake in Costa Rica is the Boa Constrictor. It is non-venomous but has an equally effective method of killing its prey. After initially grasping an animal with the pin-sharp teeth that line its jaws, the snake wraps its thick body around the animal and begins to squeeze. Each time the animal exhales, the snake further constricts its body to prevent the animal inflating its lungs with more air. The prey quickly suffocates.

The Boa Constrictor has an average length of 2–3 m, though individuals 5 m long have been recorded. It is a member of the Boidae family, which also includes the gigantic anacondas of South America. In Costa Rica, Boa Constrictors are common in dry forests and rainforests around the country, though like most snakes they are rarely seen because of their camouflaged skin. They hunt by curling up among dead leaves or between the buttress roots of a tree and ambushing an animal when it walks by. They will often choose to wait next to a watering hole or the opening to a mammal's underground burrow to improve their chances of an encounter. Boas have heat-sensitive cells on their lips that allow them to detect the body warmth of their prey. They feed on mice, rats, squirrels, raccoons, coatis, monkeys, birds and lizards as large as iguanas. In between feeding they often coil themselves in the foliage of a tree while they digest their latest meal – which may take two weeks or more.

Two other, smaller boa species live in Costa Rica. The Common Tree Boa (*Corallus ruschenbergerii*) inhabits the Osa Peninsula, and the Annulated Tree Boa (*Corallus annulatus*) lives in the rainforests of the Caribbean slope. Both species are arboreal and hunt in the same way as the Boa Constrictor.

A small number of other snakes in Costa Rica also constrict their prey as boas do. The Mussurana (*Clelia clelia*) is a very large, black snake from lowland rainforests that feeds mainly on other snakes. It delivers a vicious bite to the head of its victim before wrapping its body around it. As the Mussurana

constricts its body, it injects the other snake with venom that paralyzes it. The Neotropical Rat Snake (*Senticolis triaspis*) constricts the small rodents that it hunts in the tropical dry forests of north-west Costa Rica.

Venomous Snakes

A snake is usually classed as venomous if its venom can cause serious harm to humans. In Costa Rica there are nineteen such species from two very different groups: the Crotalinae subfamily, which are pit vipers, and the Elapidae family, which includes coral snakes and one species of sea snake.

Pit Vipers

Rainforests, dry forests and cloud forests in Costa Rica are home to pit vipers. All fourteen resident species can be recognized by their vertical, oval-shaped pupils and a triangular head with a small pit between each eye and nostril. In comparison with non-venomous snakes, their bodies are generally shorter and thicker. They are very difficult to see in the forest because of their camouflaged skin and mainly sedentary nature.

Pit vipers are exceptional hunters. They can locate their prey in total darkness and require less than a second to inject it with a toxin so potent that the animal can die within minutes.

ABOVE: *The Fer-de-Lance (*Bothrops asper*) bites more humans in Costa Rica than any other species of snake.*

The two small loreal pits between their eyes and nostrils help the snake to detect prey at night. They contain heat-sensitive cells that effectively give the snake a thermal image of any animal whose temperature differs from the surrounding environment. A viper can even determine the approximate size of the animal from the heat that it gives off. In conjunction with its tongue's sense of smell, the thermo-receptive pits allow the snake to accurately pinpoint its prey.

When the snake strikes, it stabs with two large frontal fangs through which venom is injected deep into the animal's body. Terrestrial vipers normally then release their prey and follow it until the animal succumbs to the effects of the venom. Arboreal species usually hold on to their prey as it dies because if they release it, the animal will fall to the ground and be very difficult to track.

Pit vipers typically hunt by sitting and waiting for suitable prey to walk or climb past them. When hungry, they will strike at animals that are small enough for them to swallow and large enough to provide them with a decent meal. They feed on lizards, frogs, mammals and birds. Some Costa Rican pit vipers are arboreal and lie coiled on a trunk, branch or among leafy

ABOVE: *The Neotropical Rattlesnake (*Crotalus durissus*) lives in the dry north-west of Costa Rica.*

foliage. The Eyelash Viper (*Bothriechis schlegelii*) is the most commonly seen arboreal species, which lives in rainforest throughout much of the country. It grows to an average length of 60 cm and individuals can have one of several very different skin colours. Many are a mottled green or brown, some are grey and one form is bright yellow. This snake can be easily recognized from the two eyelash-like scales it has above each eye. It is believed that these scales help shield the snake's eyes and prevent injury when it moves through dense vegetation.

They may also protect the snake's eyes from being scratched by a struggling prey animal that it has gripped in its jaws. The bright-green Side-striped Palm Pit Viper (*Bothriechis lateralis*) is another Costa Rican arboreal species, which lives at higher elevations than the Eyelash Viper, in montane rainforest and cloud forest.

Terrestrial pit vipers generally grow larger than those that live in trees, and some species are very large indeed. The Fer-de-Lance (*Bothrops asper*) is a common rainforest viper that grows to over 2 m and has 2.5 cm-long fangs. It can swallow mammals up to the size of a small opossum. This species is responsible for most of the snake bites that humans receive in

Costa Rica. This is because it is common on farmland and in long grass near villages and towns, and can become very aggressive when disturbed. As far as humans are concerned, the Fer-de-Lance is certainly the most dangerous large animal in Costa Rica.

Two other large, ground-living pit vipers found in Costa Rica are the Neotropical Rattlesnake, which can reach almost 2 m in length and inhabits the dry forests of north-west Costa Rica, and the Central American Bushmaster from the Caribbean lowland forests, which is known to grow to a length of as much as 3.5 m.

Coral Snakes and Similar Species

To discover a coral snake in the forest is an exciting experience. Until they move, these beautiful snakes look more like a child's toy than a living reptile. The vividly coloured rings that encircle their bodies contrast strikingly with the browns and greens of the forest floor.

The traditional red, yellow and black body rings of the coral snakes are seen in three species in Costa Rica. The Central

ABOVE: *Coral snakes such as the Bicoloured Coral Snake (*Micrurus multifasciatus*) chew a neurotoxin into prey to paralyze it.*

American Coral Snake (*Micrurus nigrocinctus*) is the most common and inhabits most low- and mid-elevation forests. Allen's Coral Snake (*Micrurus alleni*) is found in the Caribbean lowlands and Clarke's Coral Snake (*Micrurus clarki*) is a rarely seen species that has only been reported near the border with Panama. Another coral snake, the Bicoloured Coral Snake (*Micrurus multifasciatus*), lives on the Caribbean slope and has a black body with orange or red rings. All of these species grow to lengths of 70 cm–1 m.

Coral snakes feed mainly on other, smaller snakes, which they detect by 'tasting' the air with their forked tongues. They forage under the dead leaves, fallen branches and decomposing logs on the forest floor, both during the day and at night. Once a coral snake has trapped an animal in its small mouth, it secretes venom from its tiny fangs. The effect of this venom is enhanced by the snake chewing it into its victim's body. Unlike the haemotoxic venom of vipers that destroys body tissue, the venom of coral snakes contains a neurotoxin, which paralyzes muscles. The prey of coral snakes usually dies from a heart attack or because it can no longer inflate its lungs. The mouths of coral snakes are not large enough to bite a human leg or arm, so humans are normally only bitten by coral snakes if they pick them up with their hands, where the snake can bite a small fold of skin.

There are several species of non-venomous snake in Costa Rica that also have coloured bands around their bodies. The False Coral Snake (*Erythrolamprus mimus*) and the Tropical King Snake (*Lampropeltis triangulum*) both look like coral snakes upon first glance. However, a closer inspection reveals that the edges of the False Coral's bands are not as clearly defined as those of coral snakes, and the King Snake has yellow bands next to black bands, while coral snakes have yellow adjacent to red.

One venomous snake species in Costa Rica doesn't live on land, but in the ocean. The Yellow-bellied Sea Snake (*Pelamis platurus*) inhabits the Pacific coastal waters and is well adapted to life in the sea; it has a flattened, paddle-like tail for swimming and can absorb oxygen from the water through its skin, as well as breathing with its lungs as other snakes do. It feeds on small fish, killing them by biting and injecting them with a very potent neurotoxin.

The Yellow-bellied Sea Snake lives throughout the warm waters of the Indian and Pacific Oceans but is not a strong swimmer. It travels where ocean currents carry it and it is not uncommon for individuals to be washed up on a beach by a strong, incoming tide. In Costa Rica this 50 cm-long snake is seen more often on the sand than in the water. It poses very little danger to swimmers because it is seldom found very close to the shore and, like coral snakes, it has a very small mouth that cannot open wide enough to bite a human arm or leg.

MARINE TURTLES

One of the most fascinating displays of animal behaviour that can be witnessed in Costa Rica is the nest-building and egg-laying of marine turtles. Five of the world's seven species of these huge, most ancient of reptiles arrive on the country's beaches to complete the process that they and their ancestors have been repeating since before the age of the dinosaurs.

Female sea turtles mate and produce eggs about once every two to four years depending on the species. During a single

OPPOSITE: *Black Vultures (*Coragyps atratus*) watch Olive Ridley Turtles lay their eggs in the sand on Ostional Beach.*
BELOW: *A female Olive Ridley Turtle (*Lepidochelys olivacea*) leaves her buried eggs behind her and drags herself towards the ocean.*

ABOVE: *The last of a night's nesting Green Turtles (Chelonia mydas)
in Tortuguero National Park returns to the ocean at daybreak.*
BELOW: *The Critically Endangered Leatherback Turtle (Dermochelys
coriacea) nests on the Pacific and Caribbean coasts of Costa Rica.*

with sand. Once the turtle has returned to the ocean, all that remains of her visit are her tracks in the sand. Between about 50 and 70 days later, the eggs hatch, usually at night, and the hatchlings scurry towards the moonlight reflecting from the breaking surf.

Three of the species of sea turtle that nest in Costa Rica do so in groups. By far the most spectacular of these events is the arrival of Olive Ridley Turtles on the beaches of Ostional and Nancite in the north-west. Huge numbers of these turtles arrive over a period of about five days every month from August to December. At the peak of the season in October, tens of thousands of turtles appear from the sea in a single night and many individuals also lay their eggs during the day. Ostional and Nancite are two of the most important nesting sites for Olive Ridley Turtles in the world.

nesting season, many will visit the beach on several occasions to lay their eggs. Each emerges from the ocean at night, most commonly at high tide, and digs a hole in the sand to a depth of about 80 cm with her hind flippers. She then deposits her batch of between 50 and 200 eggs in the nest and covers it

In Tortuguero National Park on the Caribbean coast, approximately 2,000 Green Turtles (*Chelonia mydas*) nest each year from July to September. Smaller numbers of this species nest on several other beaches south of Tortuguero, including on the sands of Cahuita National Park.

A subspecies of the Caribbean Green Turtle, *Chelonia mydas agassizii*, has nesting grounds on beaches in the Osa Peninsula on the Pacific coast. In Costa Rica, this turtle, which is up to 1 m long, is one of the favourite foods of the Jaguar. This large cat kills female turtles on the beach and drags them into the jungle, where it hides the carcasses from scavengers and returns on subsequent days to feed. During the nesting season, Jaguar tracks are relatively common along the beaches of Tortuguero and Corcovado National Parks.

Significant numbers of the world's largest turtle nest in Costa Rica. The Leatherback Turtle (*Dermochelys coriacea*) grows to over 2 m long, and in Costa Rica

individuals weighing 500 kg have been recorded. This reptile is so strong that, when covering its nest, the vibrations it produces on the beach with its flippers can be felt several metres away.

The Leatherback Turtle is the sole member of the Dermochelyidae family and differs from other sea turtles by having a shell made of a hard, leathery skin instead of bone. Every year between 500 and 700 Leatherback Turtles nest in various locations along both coasts of Costa Rica. The majority lay their eggs in Las Baulas Marine National Park in Guanacaste between October and March and at Gandoca Manzanillo Wildlife Refuge on the Caribbean coast between February and July. Smaller numbers nest in Tortuguero and Cahuita National Parks, also from February to July. After nesting has been completed, Leatherback Turtles return to the deep waters of the ocean, where they migrate as far north as Canada and south to Chile and Argentina in between nesting seasons.

Two sea turtle species nest individually in Costa Rica and in small numbers. The Hawksbill Turtle (*Eretmochelys imbricata*) nests on several Pacific and Caribbean beaches from April to October, and the Loggerhead Turtle (*Caretta caretta*) nests on the Caribbean coast during these same months.

The Hawksbill is a small species that has an average length of about 80 cm. It can be easily identified by its upper jaw, which curves downwards like a parrot's beak, and its beautifully patterned shell. It inhabits mainly shallow waters, especially around coral and rocky reefs, where it feeds on molluscs, sponges and fish. It also eats jellyfish, including the highly poisonous Portuguese Man O' War (*Physalia physalis*).

The Loggerhead Turtle is the world's largest bone-shelled turtle; adults often grow to more than 1 m in length and can weigh in excess of 200 kg.

All of the five sea turtle species that nest in Costa Rica are now classed as Endangered or Critically Endangered on the Red List of Threatened Species that is published by the International Union for the Conservation of Nature and Natural Resources (IUCN).

Despite the admirable efforts and significant achievements of the Costa Rican government and sea turtle conservation groups such as the Leatherback Trust, Caribbean Conservation Corporation and the Association ANAI, the populations of these ancient reptiles that visit the country are now smaller than ever before.

ABOVE: *A newly hatched Green Turtle* (Chelonia mydas) *arrives safely at the surf.*

Turtles continue to be threatened by a number of different human activities in Costa Rica. Poachers still illegally kill females on the beaches of protected areas for their meat and steal the eggs from their nests; both are then sold in towns and cities as delicacies. A significant number of turtles drown offshore in fishing nets or die after eating floating plastic bags that they mistake for jellyfish, which are their natural prey. The building of hotels and luxury homes close to nesting beaches creates light pollution that dissuades turtles from coming ashore and, despite the benefits of ecotourism, if tourists don't remain a respectful distance from emerging turtles they return to the sea without laying their eggs.

BIRDS

Wherever you go in Costa Rica there are birds. They dive into the oceans, dash along the beaches, wade through marshes, swoop and sing in the forest, hop around active volcanic craters and even appear from nowhere to peck at your sandwich crumbs on the bleak and blustery summit of Costa Rica's highest peak.

Roughly 860 bird species live in Costa Rica for at least part of every year, and they constitute a fascinating group of hugely different birds. Compare the 2 g male Scintillant Hummingbird (*Selasphorus scintilla*) with the 7.5 kg bulk of the Harpy Eagle (*Harpia harpyja*), the high-speed Peregrine Falcon (*Falco peregrinus*) with the almost flightless Great Curassow (*Crax rubra*), and the elaborate camouflage of the Great Potoo with the flamboyant plumage of the Scarlet Macaw.

Hikers watching birds in any of Costa Rica's protected wildernesses will see and hear a whole range of shapes, colours and sounds that stir feelings of wonder, excitement and joy. Their behaviour is another source of fascination; there are hummingbirds that fly so fast their wings become invisible to the human eye, eagles that can snatch a monkey from a tree and oropendulas that weave a 2 m-long nest on the end of a swaying tree branch.

Costa Rica has been populated by birds from North and South America over a period of several million years. Since arriving, many species have split into two new – though very similar – species after being separated by the formation of the central mountain range. A clear example of this is seen with the Fiery-billed Aracari (*Pteroglossus frantzii*), which lives on the Pacific slopes, and the Collared Aracari (*Pteroglossus torquatus*), which resides predominantly on the Caribbean slope. In addition, many high-elevation species have had their ranges isolated by the lowlands of Nicaragua and Panama, and as a consequence are now endemic to Costa Rica and the western extreme of Panama.

About 70 per cent of Costa Rica's birds are permanent residents; the remainder are seasonal migrants that travel mainly from their breeding grounds in North America to avoid the cold of the winter months. A small number of species also arrive from South America. In all, the number of bird species that spend at least several months every year in Costa Rica is more than the totals for the whole of Europe or North America.

HUMMINGBIRDS

The 330 species of hummingbird that exist in the world today are endemic to the Americas. They live in a whole spectrum of different habitats, from Alaska down to the southern tips of Chile and Argentina. Forty-five of these species nest in Costa Rica and a further twelve arrive as seasonal visitors. They inhabit dry forests, mangroves, rainforests, cloud forests and *paramo*.

Hummingbirds are very small, fast, acrobatic, aggressive and colourful birds. They are fascinating to watch and their names are a joy to learn. In Costa Rica there are the Green-fronted Lancebill (*Doryfera ludoviciae*), the Purple-crowned Fairy (*Heliothryx barroti*) and the Fork-tailed Emerald (*Chlorostilbon canivetii*), to name a few.

The smallest bird in Costa Rica is the Scintillant Hummingbird. It measures 6.5 cm and weighs just 2 g when fully grown, which is lighter than a Costa Rican 50 colón coin. The smallest bird in the world, the Bee Hummingbird (*Mellisuga helenae*) from Cuba, weighs only a fraction less, at 1.8 g. Several other Costa Rican species weigh less than 3 g, including the White-crested Coquette (*Lophornis adorabilis*) and the Snowcap (*Microchera albocoronata*).

Costa Rica's largest hummingbirds are the Violet Sabrewing and the White-tipped Sicklebill, both of which reach 11 g in weight and 13–15 cm in length.

The principal food of hummingbirds is nectar, which provides them with the energy they require to maintain their extremely active lifestyle. They feed almost continuously during the day, metabolizing the sugar as fast as they ingest it. Because they have almost no fat reserves, these birds live permanently on the verge of starvation. To survive the night, they do assimilate a little fat that they can burn while they sleep, and on cold evenings they enter a hibernation-like state called torpor that slows down their metabolism and the burning of energy reserves.

In order to extract nectar from flowers, hummingbirds normally have to remain in the air. This is because their weight, however low, prevents them from landing directly on most flowers. Their wings differ from those of other birds in that they have no elbow joint but instead possess extremely manoeuvrable shoulder joints that allow the wing to turn on its axis through almost 180 degrees. Such a design allows the birds to fly backwards and obtain lift from both the down- and

OPPOSITE: *A Green Violet-ear (*Colibri thalassinus*) feeding on the high-altitude ginger plant* Costus montanus.

rich nectar. The form of the bill of a hummingbird dictates which flowers the bird can most easily feed from; a long, curved bill can access flowers that are often curved themselves and have nectar hidden deep inside them. The Hermits and Violet Sabrewing all have beaks of this type and are common visitors to the curved flowers of heliconias. Shorter, straighter beaks are more common and are more appropriate for small, delicate flowers, and such bills are seen in the Fiery-throated Hummingbird (*Panterpe insignis*) and the Green Thorntail (*Discosura conversii*).

Feeding strategies vary among hummingbirds. Some aggressive males hold small territories. Less aggressive species sneak in and out of those territories, and others have designated foraging routes that run for kilometres through a forest. As well as feeding at flowers, all hummingbirds supplement their diets with insects and spiders, which provide important proteins and nutrients not found in nectar.

The gaudy, iridescent feathers of hummingbirds are not the result of chemical pigments as is the case with other birds. Hummingbird colours are 'physical colours', which means they are caused by the selective reflection of light from the physical structure of the feather. Some wavelengths (colours) are reflected successfully and others are not. The colour can also only be seen when viewed from certain angles; a phenomenon that can make photographing these birds quite a challenge. When done well, however, images that show off the deep purple of the Violet Sabrewing, the greens and blues of the Green Violet-ear (*Colibri thalassinus*) and the bright orange of the female Purple-throated Mountaingem (*Lampornis calolaema*) are spectacular.

ABOVE: *A Long-tailed Hermit (*Phaethornis superciliosus*) arriving at its nest.*

upstrokes when hovering. The agility that this gives the birds is essential for their unique method of feeding.

If a flower is very sturdy – for example a heliconia – the hummingbird may land and feed on foot, using its wings just for balance. This is the preferred feeding technique of the Green-crowned Brilliant (*Heliodoxa jacula*).

When hummingbirds feed in mid-flight, they rapidly flick their elongated tongue in and out of the flower to extract the

Female hummingbirds work without the direct help of the male to build their nests. They use cobwebs to bind together a mixture of lichen, grass, moss and dead leaves, which they build on a branch or the upper surface of a leaf. These materials help to camouflage the nest from snakes, coatis, squirrels and birds such as toucans that all predate hummingbird nests. The small, cup-shaped nest will typically hold two eggs that hatch after two to three weeks of incubation. The young are ready to leave the nest between eighteen and twenty-eight days later. Hermit hummingbirds build their nests in a slightly different way, constructing a funnel-shaped nest that hangs from the tip of a palm or heliconia leaf. The female sits guard at the entrance to the nest with her head and tail feathers protruding from the hole.

In Costa Rica, hummingbirds can be seen in almost every habitat and year round. Their lives obviously revolve around feeding at nectar-rich flowers, so their appearance will depend on the blooming of these flowers. Generally, most lowland species of hummingbird nest during the dry season when there are more blooms. In many highland areas, nesting occurs more frequently during the rainy season for the same reason.

THE TROGON FAMILY

Trogons (family Trogonidae) are found in tropical forests around the world, and ten species live in Costa Rica. Their multi-coloured plumage is a grand display of natural beauty. Each species and gender can be distinguished by the different colours on its head, eye-ring and belly, as well as by the absence or pattern of bars on its tail feathers.

Trogons can be found countrywide though most species have their own limited range. The Lattice-tailed Trogon (*Trogon clathratus*) is a resident of the Caribbean foothills, the Black-headed Trogon rarely strays out of the dry north-west and the Collared Trogon (*Trogon collaris*) inhabits the mid to high elevations of the Central and Talamanca mountain ranges. One species that can be found in almost all regions of the country is the Violaceous Trogon (*Trogon violaceus*).

Trogons are very sedate birds, so despite their bright colours they are difficult to spot in the forest until they take to the air or begin to call. They feed predominantly on insects and fruits, which they snatch from twigs, branches or the forest floor without landing. When a trogon discovers a bunch of ripe berries, it flies repeatedly back and forth from a nearby perch, taking a single fruit at a time.

The preferred nesting site for trogons is a decaying tree trunk. Both the male and female of a mating pair of birds work together to carve out a hole in the tree with their bills. Alternatively, if they find a suitable abandoned nest-hole they will use that. They take turns incubating the eggs and once the chicks hatch, both parents fetch food for their offspring.

The most famous member of the Costa Rican trogon family is the Resplendent Quetzal. The male is considered the most ornately decorated and beautiful bird in Central America. Its ruffled head feathers, striking red breast and long, flowing, emerald tail feathers that can grow to 75 cm in length give it a

ABOVE, RIGHT: *The Rufous-tailed Hummingbird (*Amazilia tzacatl*) prefers non-forest habitats and is a common visitor to gardens.*
RIGHT: *The Slaty-tailed Trogon (*Trogon massena*) lives mainly in the rainforest of the Caribbean lowlands and foothills.*

ABOVE: *A female Resplendent Quetzal (*Pharomachrus mocinno*) arrives at her nest-hole in a cloud forest tree trunk.*
LEFT: *The male Resplendent Quetzal was revered by the Mayan and Aztec civilizations because of its beauty.*

majestic appearance that few other birds in the world can match. The bird was sacred to the Mayan and Aztec people of Central America, and today it is celebrated by Guatemalans as their national bird and the name of their currency.

Resplendent Quetzals breed in the cool and damp cloud forests of Costa Rica's mountain ranges. Their mating and feeding behaviour is very similar to that of the trogons. They nest in hollow trees and the male and female are equally involved in the parental care of the eggs and chicks. During this period they feed heavily on little avocado fruits (*Ocotea tonduzii*), which they pluck from the canopy in mid-flight. After the mating season quetzals migrate down the mountain slopes – there is more food available there during the wetter months of July to February.

The Resplendent Quetzal has become seriously endangered in recent years because of the deforestation of its lowland feeding grounds. More frequent high winds over the Continental Divide, blamed partly on deforestation on the Pacific slopes, also pose a threat to its existence because they blow down the decaying tree trunks in which it makes its nests.

ABOVE: *The enormous bill of an adult Keel-billed Toucan* (Ramphastos sulfuratus) *is light and manoeuvrable, despite its size.*

TOUCANS

The huge-billed toucans nest inside living or dead tree trunks. However, in contrast to trogons and despite their large beaks, they don't make the holes themselves. Instead, they search for old woodpecker nests, or natural cavities in decaying wood that provide enough room for them and their brood.

Six species of the neotropical toucan family Ramphastidae live in the mid-elevation and lowland forests of Costa Rica. They are all timid birds that prefer to forage up in the canopy, often in small, loose flocks of between four and fifteen individuals. They are frugivorous, but will also occasionally eat small reptiles, eggs and chicks.

Their trademark, enlarged bill is the most colourful of all Costa Rican birds' bills. The largest species, the Chestnut-mandibled Toucan and the Keel-billed Toucan, have bills that measure up to 25 cm in length, which can be half as long as their bodies. The outer surface of the bill is made of layers of keratin, the same material that forms nails and horns. Inside, there is an air-filled, foam-like matrix of bone filaments. The overall structure is extremely strong yet very light and accounts for only approximately 5 per cent of the bird's overall weight.

A toucan's bill has a variety of different functions. Its large size is extremely effective when reaching for fruits at the very ends of branches or plucking chicks from inside nest-holes. The colourful bill also plays an important role in mating displays, and can be used effectively when the bird has to defend its nest from a predator.

Aracaris are medium-sized toucans that have narrower bills than their larger relatives and bright red and orange stripes across their belly that look almost like a hand-knitted sweater. In Costa Rica, the Collared Aracari is found almost exclusively on the Caribbean slope, and the range of the Fiery-billed Aracari is restricted to the Pacific side of the country's mountain ranges. These two species originated from two populations of a single species that were separated by the rise of the Talamanca mountain range millions of years ago. Unlike the rest of the toucans, adult and fledgling aracaris roost together in nest-holes in groups of up to five or six individuals. This helps to conserve body warmth and provides more defence against predators.

The smallest toucan species in Costa Rica are the vibrant Emerald Toucanet, which is common in all mid-elevation rainforests of both slopes, and the Yellow-eared Toucanet (*Selenidera spectabilis*), which lives in forests on the Caribbean and north Pacific foothills.

ABOVE: *A Scarlet Macaw (Ara macao) lifts off from a tree in Corcovado National Park.*

MACAWS

Macaws are highly sociable birds. These large, long-tailed parrots are monogamous and usually forage in family groups that unite to form flocks of between ten and twenty-five birds. When feeding, they use their strong, hooked bills to tear open the fruits and nuts they pick from the canopy. The falling of husks and other discarded vegetation from the canopy is often the first sign one notices of a group of feeding macaws.

The Scarlet Macaw and the Great Green Macaw (*Ara ambigua*) are well documented in Costa Rica for their exceptional beauty and their struggle for survival. They are truly magnificent birds that command a presence in the forest canopy that is surpassed by no other species. Their large size, brightly coloured plumage and raucous nature can provide a most memorable bird-watching or photographing experience.

The wild populations of macaws in Costa Rica have been decimated by the destruction of their habitats, by hunting and by the poaching of their eggs and chicks for the pet trade. The Scarlet Macaw was common along both coastlines in the early 1900s, but is now restricted to the central and south Pacific coasts, with a few mating pairs remaining in the dry forests of

Guanacaste. In an effort to save these birds, the Zoo Ave Foundation has operated a highly successful breeding and release programme for Scarlet Macaws on the Osa Peninsula since 1998. By the beginning of 2007, a total of 86 macaws had been raised by the project's organizers.

The Great Green Macaw relies heavily on the gigantic Tonka Bean Tree (*Dipteryx panamensis*) as a source of food and for nesting. Regrettably, this species has been felled in large numbers for its valuable, hard wood. As a result, the Great Green Macaw now only inhabits isolated areas of the northern Caribbean lowlands between Braulio Carrillo National Park and the Nicaraguan border. These areas represent only a tenth of the land that their former range covered.

In 2001, the San Juan-La Selva Biological Corridor project was initiated by the Rainforest Biodiversity Group with the aim of protecting the 262,000 hectares of lowland forest that joins the River San Juan on the Nicaraguan border with the world-famous biological station La Selva and the adjacent Braulio Carrillo National Park.

In 2006 the project received a $50,000 grant from the US Fish and Wildlife Service to help create six new private reserves along the route. These new reserves will be linked to the existing reserves, and the entire corridor is expected to be complete and open to visitors in 2008.

BIRDS OF PREY

From the shadows of a gloomy jungle understorey or from a treetop high above the ground, birds of prey calmly watch the forests, marshes, grasslands and coastlines of Costa Rica for signs of movement. The sixty-four species of the order Falconiformes that live in Costa Rica include eagles, falcons, hawks, kites, vultures and caracaras. Their prey ranges in size from camouflaged insects on the forest floor to fully grown sloths in the canopy.

Because food is so abundant in the tropics, some birds of prey have become very specialized hunters. The Laughing Falcon (*Herpetotheres cachinnans*) feeds almost exclusively on snakes, which it swoops down onto and immobilizes with its talons. It then kills the snake by biting the back of its head and carries it off to a perch to eat. The diet of the Snail Kite (*Rostrhamus sociabilis*) consists mainly of large snails. It flies close to the surface of freshwater marshes and snatches the snails from the shallows without landing. The bird's long and sharply hooked beak enables it to easily extract the snail from its shell.

The Tiny Hawk (*Accipiter superciliosus*) is the smallest of Costa Rica's birds of prey. Females grow to 26 cm and males to only 20 cm, which enables them to easily hide in vegetation and ambush small birds such as hummingbirds. In contrast,

ABOVE: *The Turkey Vulture (*Cathartes aura*) has a powerful sense of smell and can detect carrion from hundreds of metres up in the air.*

Costa Rica's largest bird of prey, the Harpy Eagle, reaches 1 m in height and can weigh 7.5 kg. It feeds on arboreal mammals such as sloths and monkeys, which it snatches from the tree-tops with powerful, 12 cm-long talons. It then lifts off with thrusts from its 1 m-long wings, carrying the stunned prey. Ironically, this robust and fearsome bird of prey remains on the verge of extinction in Costa Rica because of hunting and the destruction of its habitat. Sporadic sightings of the Harpy Eagle over recent years on the Osa Peninsula have maintained the hope that it hasn't disappeared and may yet make a comeback.

An extremely important role in the food chain of tropical habitats is played by vultures and caracaras. All these birds are very common in Costa Rica, where they efficiently dispose of carrion in forests, on open land and along beaches. The Turkey Vulture (*Cathartes aura*) is almost always the first to arrive at a carcass because of its exceptionally keen sense of smell. It can detect rotting meat through a dense forest canopy and pin-points the source by gliding in ever-decreasing circles. The presence of a Turkey Vulture on the ground will always attract Black Vultures, which appear to have a very limited sense of smell themselves but very sharp eyesight. The larger and much

ABOVE: *The Little Blue Heron* (Egretta caerulea) *uses its long neck and bill to strike at fish that swim past it.*

Once the sun has set and darkness falls, owls take over from the diurnal birds of prey. Thirteen species from the family Strigidae live in Costa Rica, where they hunt rodents, bats, birds and insects in a variety of habitats including forests, forest clearings, savannah, coffee plantations and pastures. The Great Horned Owl (*Bubo virginianus*) is the largest and reaches a height of about 50 cm in the tropics. Its body size and large, upright ear tufts distinguish it from other owls in Costa Rica.

In all owls, one ear is positioned slightly higher and further forwards than the other, which means that one ear will hear a sound fractionally before the other. This enables the owl to pinpoint the source of a sound made by its prey more accurately. The bird then swoops down on the animal, which it can do almost in silence because of its fluffy flight feathers that produce almost no sound as the bird beats its wings.

The smallest owl in Costa Rica is the Least Pygmy Owl (*Glaucidium minutissimum*), which measures just 14 cm when fully grown. Like other pygmy owls, it is highly dextrous and can snatch small birds, lizards and insects from trees, which it often does during the day. It lives exclusively on the Caribbean slope, where it nests in old woodpecker holes in the canopy.

WATER BIRDS

The permanent and seasonal aquatic habitats in Costa Rica draw a plethora of birds to their waters, where an abundance of food is available.

The seasonal marshes of the Río Frío region in the north and the Río Tempisque watershed in Guanacaste swell with birdlife during the end of the wet season and the onset of the dry season. Among the thousands of ducks, herons, storks, ibises and egrets that assemble stands the tallest bird in Costa Rica, the Jabiru. Its 1.5-m frame looms over the water through which it wades, stabbing at mud-eels, fish and amphibians with its 30 cm-long upturned beak. The Jabiru also helps to keep the water clean because it feeds on fish that die when a lagoon dries up. The Jabiru is easily distinguished from a similar-looking species, the Wood Stork, by the bright red feathers on its throat. In the air it can be identified by its very slow, graceful wing beats.

In the Río Tempisque basin the Jabiru has become almost extinct, with perhaps as few as fifty individuals remaining. The conversion of wooded areas to rice and sugarcane plantations has severely reduced the number of large trees in which these birds can nest, and forest fires have destroyed established nests that had been used for years. In addition, chicks are sometimes stolen from their nests and sold to unscrupulous buyers.

Roseate Spoonbills add a splash of colour to the marshes and lagoons of Costa Rica. The bright-pink colour of these wading birds comes from a carotenoid pigment obtained from some of the invertebrates that they eat. The same pigment is also responsible for the colouration of flamingos, carp and salmon. Because the water of lagoons is usually muddy, spoon-

more colourful King Vulture will also investigate the activity on the ground and the other birds will move aside for it. The King Vulture is quite a shy bird that normally perches in the top of the canopy or soars high in the air. It is much more wary of humans than the Turkey and Black Vultures.

The Crested Caracara will also join vultures to feed and despite its smaller size, can drive away a single Black or Turkey Vulture. This bird also hunts live lizards, snakes and small mammals, usually on foot.

During the nesting seasons of marine turtles in Costa Rica, Black Vultures, Turkey Vultures and Crested Caracaras all assemble on the beach to search for hatchlings, eggs that are uncovered by the tide and females that become too exhausted to return to the sea.

bills feed by touch rather than sight. They swing their open, spoon-shaped bills through the water, creating turbulence that lifts small animals from the sediment into the water. When the bird feels an object enter its beak, a reflex reaction makes it snap shut.

Some birds have developed extremely long toes and claws to facilitate walking on top of floating vegetation in ponds and lagoons. The Purple Gallinule is a stocky aquatic bird with violet and green body plumage, bright yellow legs and a red and yellow bill. Its huge feet provide the balance it needs to walk from one floating leaf to another as it picks water lily fruits, aquatic insects and small frogs from the water.

The Northern Jacana performs the same balancing act with its elongated toes. It is fairly abundant in the wetlands of Costa Rica, and its harsh, chattering call is one of the most commonly heard sounds. This species is polyandrous, which means that the female mates with more than one male within a territory that she defends. The males incubate the eggs without help from the female and then care for the chicks when they are born. Polyandry is uncommon in the animal world, although it is observed in some other species of bird, primate, insect and fish.

The rivers, streams and canals of Costa Rica are popular feeding sites for herons, kingfishers, bitterns, Anhingas (*Anhinga anhinga*) and cormorants.

The Great Blue Heron (*Ardea herodias*) is the largest of its family, and can reach an impressive height of 130 cm. It is a shy bird that stands patiently in the shallows waiting to ambush passing fish. Its extremely long neck gives it plenty of reach when it stabs at prey with its bill. Most other heron species hunt in this manner, combining stealth with lethal speed. Boat journeys along the rivers of Costa Rica will provide glimpses of species such as the Green-backed Heron, the Chestnut-bellied Heron (*Agamia agami*), the Little Blue Heron (*Egretta caerulea*) and the nocturnal Boat-billed Heron (*Cochlearius cochlearius*) perched on branches over the water or patrolling the muddy banks.

The large Bare-throated Tiger Heron is one of the most commonly seen herons in Costa Rica. Its finely barred plumage camouflages it well against the vegetation as it quietly stalks fish in rivers and lagoons. It can also be extremely boisterous, however. When surprised, it emits a loud and recurring 'honk', and at dawn and dusk males often produce a loud roar that can be quite startling for a photographer or bird-watcher crouched in the semi-darkness.

Many birds inhabit the shorelines of Costa Rica, where they find a wealth of food in the ocean, estuaries and mangroves, and on mud flats, sand bars and beaches. Plovers, Whimbrels, godwits, turnstones, sandpipers and yellowlegs are all migrant visitors to the coasts of Costa Rica during the winter months, where they feed on crustaceans, molluscs, insects, algae and marine worms in the substrate.

Brown Boobies (*Sula leucogaster*) and Magnificent Frigatebirds (*Fregata magnificens*) nest on islands situated close to the shore, the Blue-footed Booby (*Sula nebouxii*) ranges further out to sea, while the Red-footed Booby (*Sula sula*) and the Masked Booby (*Sula dactylatra*) are two of the thirteen species of bird that nest on Costa Rica's Cocos Island, located in the Pacific Ocean.

OTHER BIRDS

There are of course many other species of bird in Costa Rica from a range of different orders and families that are of great interest. They all vary greatly in their appearance and behaviour, and all bring excitement and splendour to the wilds of

BELOW: *The ground-dwelling Great Curassow (*Crax rubra*) – a male is shown here – stands almost a metre tall and can weigh 4 kg.*

Costa Rica. The Great Curassow is a very large, pheasant-like bird that spends almost all of its life in the shadows of the rainforest floor. The male is almost all black with a bright yellow knob on the top of its beak. The female is a reddish-brown colour. These birds wander slowly through the undergrowth in mating pairs or family groups of up to six individuals. Because of their slow movements and dark colours they are hard to detect, which is their best defence against predators. If they are threatened, however, they will fly up onto a low perch in a bluster of flapping wings until the danger has passed.

Another bird that relies on camouflage to evade predators is the Great Potoo (*Nyctibius grandis*). In Costa Rica it resides in the lowland rainforests of the Caribbean slope and on the Osa Peninsula. During the day it sleeps perched on a tree branch or stump. Its plumage closely resembles the colour and texture of tree bark, making the bird extremely difficult to detect, even at close range. At night the Great Potoo hunts flying insects and sometimes small bats.

A very similar, smaller species, the Common Potoo (*Nyctibius griseus*), is also found in Costa Rica, throughout the lowlands and foothills of both slopes.

Some of the most spectacular bird nests in Costa Rica are built by the oropendolas. The huge, hanging nests of the Montezuma Oropendola and the smaller Chestnut-headed Oropendola (*Psarocolius wagleri*) are a fairly common sight at low elevations on the Caribbean slope. Dozens of these nests can be seen adorning the branches of a single tree – the chosen tree is typically very tall and separated from the dense canopy. The Montezuma Oropendola nest is the largest and can be 2 m in length. The female begins weaving the nest at the very end of a branch in order to dissuade the approach of climbing predators, even though this means that the nest swings precariously in strong winds. She gradually works downwards, creating a tubular structure that she closes off at the bottom. The entrance to the nest is at the top and the eggs lie on a cluster of dead leaves at the bottom.

Though unmolested by most predators, the nests of oropendolas are parasitized by the Giant Cowbird (*Scaphidura oryzivora*), which lays its eggs among the oropendola's own brood. These foreign eggs are cared for and the chicks fed by the oropendola, thus releasing the Giant Cowbird from the costly obligations of parental care.

Male Montezuma Oropendolas can be easily identified by two of their calls. One sounds like the ripping of cloth, and the most spectacular, saved for the mating display, is a gurgling sound that ends in a high-pitched note as the male rocks forwards on a perch with his wings held high.

The Scarlet-rumped Cacique (*Cacicus uropygialis*) and the Streak-backed Oriole are two smaller Costa Rican birds that

LEFT: *A Montezuma Oropendola (*Psarocolius montezuma*) flies from its enormous hanging nest, which can measure 2 m long.*

also weave hanging nests, though of a more modest size.

One Costa Rican bird family adds a wider variety of colours to the forests than any other. The tanagers, or Thraupidae, are small, sparrow-sized birds that are all but unique to the New World tropics. The family includes the honeycreepers and the euphonias. Their plumages combine the more modest colours of black, grey, brown and white with vivid shades of red, blue, violet, yellow, green or orange. Costa Rica has fifty members of this family, almost all of which are residents. Collectively, they inhabit forests from the coast all the way up to the tree line where the *paramo* begins. One

species, the Black-cheeked Ant Tanager (*Habia atrimaxillares*), is endemic to the country and is now only found in the South Pacific lowlands. Tanagers are extremely active birds that hop and flutter from tree to tree, feeding on seeds, fruits, nectar, flowers and the occasional insect. They sometimes travel as part of a mixed-species flock that moves through the vegetation consuming almost everything edible in its path. The different species within the flock normally eat different food and so do not compete with each other. It is believed that each bird that joins the group benefits by having more eyes around it to watch for predators and therefore can spend more time feeding and less time looking around. It is also possible that fruit-eating birds help flush out more insects for the insectivorous species.

The Red-throated Ant-Tanager (*Habia fuscicauda*) and the Black-cheeked Ant-Tanager will occasionally form part of a mixed-species flock that follows an army ant swarm, snapping up the insects that run, jump and fly from the advancing ants. Other, larger birds are also attracted by the commotion. Both the Blue-crowned Motmot (*Momotus momota*) and the Rufous Motmot (*Baryphthengus martii*) perch in shadows close to the ground and fly short, sudden sorties to snatch fleeing insects, spiders and frogs. These birds can be clearly distinguished by their two long tail feathers that have no barbs along part of their length and sport a racket-shaped tip. Barbs do form along the entire length of the shaft when the bird is young but – apart from those at the tip – they are weakly attached and later fall off. Both males and females flick their pendulum-like tails from side to side when perched. This may be a way of warning predators that the bird has spotted them and in the case of males it could also play a part in their courtship displays.

ABOVE: *The Speckled Tanager (*Tangara guttata*) is one of 50 members of the tanager family (*Thraupidae*) inhabiting Costa Rica.* BELOW: *The Blue-crowned Motmot (*Momotus momota*) follows army ant swarms, feeding on small animals escaping the insects.*

Mammals

It is always a special moment when we encounter a wild mammal in its natural habitat. As we are mammals too, we feel we can understand its behaviour better than that of any bird, reptile or smaller organism. Within the small territory of Costa Rica there are 240 species of mammal, which represent 6 per cent of all the mammal species in the world. Despite such a high diversity, however, encounters with many of these species are quite rare, for which there are two reasons. Firstly, almost all are wary of humans and have well-developed senses that they can use to avoid us if they wish. Secondly, the majority are nocturnal and many also live in the trees where they are easily obscured by vegetation.

In many cases, mammals in Costa Rica are detected by the tracks they leave behind in the sand or mud rather than actually being seen. During turtle-nesting seasons the paw prints of Jaguars and Ocelots become quite common along the beaches in Corcovado, Tortuguero and Santa Rosa National Parks. A multitude of White-nosed Coati and raccoon prints also zigzag across large stretches of sand. In the forest, many manmade trails are followed or crossed by mammals that leave their footprints in the soft mud. Very early morning is a great time to search for these, before other walkers or rainfall erases the signs of the night's activity.

Mammals play a valuable role in the ecosystems in which they live. Many herbivores are important seed dispersers, and a number of bats are the sole pollinators of the flowers they feed on. Carnivores help control the populations of the smaller animals in their habitat, and those mammals that feed on carrion reduce the proliferation of diseases from rotting corpses.

BAIRD'S TAPIR

The Baird's Tapir is the largest land animal in Costa Rica, and of all the mammals in the neotropical rainforests it is only exceeded in size by the Brazilian Tapir (*Tapirus terrestris*) of South America.

The sound of a tapir stomping through the undergrowth can be quite an unnerving experience before the animal comes into view. A fully grown Baird's Tapir is the size of a small donkey, and its feet with their enormous toes leave 15 cm-wide depressions in the soil. It stands 1 m high at the shoulder, measures 2 m from nose to tail and can reach a weight of up to 250 kg.

Fortunately for wildlife-watchers, tapirs are strictly herbivorous and spend many hours of each day grazing on fallen fruits, shrubs and small trees. It is not uncommon for a healthy tapir to ingest between 30 and 40 kg of vegetation in a day. To help them in this impressive feat, tapirs have an elongated, prehensile snout that they use to grasp leaves or whole plants and pull them into their mouth. This proboscis can also bend upwards, which provides the animal with a little extra reach when feeding on shrubs or the low branches of trees.

In Costa Rica tapirs live in large tracts of undisturbed forest and on the open *paramo* in Chirripó National Park. Like many other large mammals they have an affinity with water and will often swim or even submerge themselves in slow-flowing rivers to cool down on hot days. Tapirs are competent swimmers and will not hesitate to cross a small river in order to feed on the opposite bank or to escape a predator.

The only natural predator that adult tapirs have is the Jaguar, though their young may also be attacked by smaller wild cats such as the Puma and the Ocelot. Baby tapirs have brown fur with white lines and spots, which makes them very difficult to distinguish from the undergrowth when the animal stays still. To remain motionless is therefore their best defence against cats, which predominantly rely on their eyesight and hearing when hunting.

Unlike cats, tapirs have very poor eyesight and depend on their smell and hearing to assess their surroundings. Their vision is so bad that I have twice had wild Baird's Tapirs come within centimetres of me in the rainforest as I was photographing them.

As a result of their very limited eyesight, Baird's Tapirs are easy prey for hunters. Despite the relative protection that national parks provide them, these animals are still shot for sport and as reprisals by hunters who have been prosecuted by the authorities for hunting.

Tapirs usually produce just a single calf from each thirteen-month pregnancy, which makes it impossible for a population

OPPOSITE: *With a weight of up to 250 kg, the endangered Baird's Tapir (*Tapirus bairdii*) is Costa Rica's largest land mammal.*

ABOVE: *A female Collared Peccary (*Tayassu tajacu*) leads her young through a rainforest clearing.*

to recover its numbers quickly. As a result of overhunting and also habitat destruction, it is unlikely that more than several hundred Baird's Tapirs now remain in Costa Rica.

PECCARIES

Peccaries are wild, pig-like animals with dark, wiry fur and large, triangular-shaped heads. They belong to the Tayassuidae family and are most closely related to true pigs and hippopotamuses, with which they share the suborder Suiformes. In Costa Rica they live in the forest in herds of varying sizes and are most easily recognized by the pungent odour they produce from their anal glands to mark their territory; during most encounters with humans they are smelt long before they are actually seen.

Two species of peccary live in Costa Rica: the very rare White-lipped Peccary and the much more common Collared Peccary.

The White-lipped Peccary is the slightly larger of the two with an average body length of 1 m. It also has longer, shaggy hair along the top of its back that stands on end when the ani-

mal is startled. The White-lipped Peccary is renowned for forming large herds and for its reportedly aggressive nature. Individuals usually live in groups of between 50 and 100 individuals, though herds of more than 250 have been recorded. Because of hunting and habitat destruction, this species is now very rare in Costa Rica and is only found in large numbers in Corcovado National Park. Much smaller populations exist in the Caribbean rainforest of La Amistad National Park and Barra del Colorado Wildlife Refuge.

White-lipped Peccaries feed on fruits, seeds, roots, tubers, grasses and invertebrates, especially earthworms. They travel extensively throughout the year, following the availability of these different food types. Their diet therefore dictates that they require extremely large home ranges located in undisturbed, productive forest.

In Corcovado National Park these peccaries are the favourite food of Jaguars. Pumas and Ocelots will also occasionally feed on them. When alarmed by the approach of a wild cat or a human being, peccaries snort and click their teeth together very loudly. If the intruder persists, the whole herd then begins to run. To be close to one of these thunderous stampedes in the forest can be quite frightening, especially as it can be difficult to determine which way the peccaries are

running at first. The frequently quoted advice of climbing a tree should be heeded by anyone who finds themselves at the front of one of these galloping herds.

If a White-lipped Peccary is separated from its herd and cornered by a cat it has a fearsome method of defence; it has four very sharp, 4 cm-long canine teeth with which it can deliver a vicious bite. Alone, it represents a dangerous opponent, and if other peccaries come to its aid the cat is wise to retreat.

The Collared Peccary is less aggressive than the White-lipped Peccary and a little more tolerant of humans. It lives in much smaller groups, which rarely exceed thirty individuals. This species has a light grey band around its neck, which helps to distinguish it from the White-lipped Peccary.

Collared Peccaries are common in many of Costa Rica's national parks and reserves, where they inhabit dry forest, rainforest and cloud forest environments. They seem a little less sensitive to habitat destruction than White-lipped Peccaries because they do not have such large home ranges.

SLOTHS

When a sloth is in a hurry it can travel about 5 m in a minute. If, however, it is not being stalked by a predator or chased out

ABOVE: *The Brown-throated Three-toed Sloth (*Bradypus variegatus*) may walk along the ground if unable to find a way via the canopy.*

of another sloth's territory, then a sloth on the move will cover about 2–3 m every minute. For this reason, and because they are usually not moving at all, it is quite difficult to spot a sloth in the forest. Nevertheless, these animals are one of the most widely distributed and common large mammals in the neotropics.

Two of the world's six species of sloth live in Costa Rica. The Brown-throated Three-toed Sloth and Hoffman's Two-toed Sloth are found countrywide on both Caribbean and Pacific slopes and are only absent on the *paramo* and in some of the highest cloud forests. The drastic decline in the numbers of Jaguars and Harpy Eagles, which are the main natural predators of sloths, has meant that large populations of these sloths remain within the protected wild areas in Costa Rica.

These two sloth species are physically quite different. The Three-toed Sloth has three large claws on its forefeet and the Two-toed Sloth has, as you would expect, just two. The Three-toed has darker fur than the Two-toed, and the pattern of colours on its face provides the impression that it is permanently smiling. Male Three-toed Sloths can additionally be

ABOVE: *A baby Brown-throated Three-toed Sloth (*Bradypus variegatus) *clings to its mother's stomach high in the canopy.*

identified by the black and yellow patch of fur in the centre of their back.

Though both species are equally common in Costa Rica, one can have the impression that Three-toed Sloths are more numerous because they are diurnal – the Two-toed Sloth is only usually active at night.

The highly lethargic lifestyle of sloths is a consequence of their diet. They feed almost entirely on leaves, which provide the animal with very little energy and sometimes require up to a month to digest. Sloths therefore have an exceptionally slow metabolism that does not allow for fast body movements or anything more than short periods of physical activity. The body temperature of the Two-toed Sloth can drop as low as 25°C, which is the lowest of any active mammal. To partly compensate, both sloth species sunbathe in order to heat up their bodies and accelerate the digestive process in their stomach.

At first glance, the sloth's long and thick fur seems inappropriate for an animal that inhabits tropical forests. However, because the animal has such a slow metabolism and hence produces little heat, the extra insulation that its coat provides is essential, especially when the temperature drops at night.

The fur also allows the sloth to dry out quickly after a rainstorm because of one unique feature; the hairs grow from the sloth's arms and legs towards its body and from its stomach round to its back. In all other land mammals the hairs grow

towards the hands and feet. Because the sloth spends most of its time hanging from branches, the direction of growth is therefore downwards, which facilitates the drainage of rainwater from the animal's body. One other peculiarity of the sloth's fur is that it is often green, in particular during the wet season. This colour is not produced by the sloth, but by microscopic algae that grow on its hairs. The sloth does not try to remove the algae, so their relationship may be symbiotic, with the algae obtaining a safe place to grow and the sloth becoming more effectively camouflaged from predators.

Despite the fact that they have much less muscle tissue than other mammals of their size, sloths are nonetheless able to grip branches and creepers with surprising force. The muscles that close their claws are so strong that they can hang upside down

ABOVE: *Usually active only at night, Hoffman's Two-toed Sloth* (Choloepus hoffmanni) *is seen less often than its three-toed cousin.*

from a branch while feeding and support their body weight with their hind feet. These long claws can also be used to slash at a predator when the sloth is attacked and, bizarrely, for swimming, which sloths are able to do quite well when the need arises.

Sloths spend almost all of their lives in trees. They are born in the canopy and inevitably take their last few breaths there too. Once a week however, they do descend to the forest floor, a habit which is quite dangerous for an animal that is preyed on by very agile wild cats but can itself only walk as fast as a tortoise. The purpose of the trip is, however, a very important

one; the sloth leaves the safety of the tree in order to urinate and defecate, which it never does while in the canopy. Various theories exist as to why sloths should do this though none have been proved. The most popular explanation suggests that the sloth is helping beetles and moths that live in its fur to complete their life cycle, with the assumption that the sloth receives some benefit from this proposed relationship. The larvae of these insects live in sloth faeces and the adults hop off their host and lay their eggs when the sloth is defecating. They then return to the sloth before it climbs back up the tree. The adult insects that emerge from the larvae in the faeces will jump onto a sloth when one next descends from a tree, thus completing the cycle.

ANTEATERS AND ARMADILLOS

Anteaters are close relatives of sloths and armadillos. They are all placed in the same superorder, Xenartha, and have enlarged claws on their front feet which they use for climbing or digging. In the case of anteaters, their claws are used for tearing open ant and termite nests.

Three species of anteater inhabit the forests of Costa Rica. The Giant Anteater stands 1 m tall at the shoulder and is by far the largest. This ground-dwelling species has thick and coarse hair and a huge bushy tail that sweeps the forest floor as it walks. Its head is long and narrow, ending in a 50 cm-long snout that is ideal for penetrating deep into ant and termite nests. Sadly, the Giant Anteater is on the brink of extinction in Costa Rica. There has been just a single confirmed sighting, in Corcovado National Park, during recent years. It is likely that Giant Anteaters will soon become unique to the South American continent.

The most common anteater in Costa Rica is the Northern Tamandua, which forages on the ground and in trees in low- and mid-elevation forests throughout the country. It is about the size of a raccoon or a badger and has black fur around its torso in the form of a waistcoat, which contrasts strongly with the yellow fur on its limbs. Its hairless tail is prehensile and provides the anteater with essential grip when climbing up and down trees.

The Silky Anteater has a similar distribution to the Northern Tamandua but is exclusively arboreal, nocturnal and much smaller than the other two species in Costa Rica. It measures just 30 cm in length, half of which is its prehensile tail.

Anteaters feed on both ants and termites. They have an exceptional sense of smell that leads them to the insects' nests, which they tear into using their strong claws. Sometimes they stand on top of the nest and dig with all four feet. After an anteater has created a hole in an ant or termite nest, it rapidly flicks its long, sticky tongue in and out of the opening. The

LEFT: *A Northern Tamandua (*Tamandua mexicana*) investigates a termite nest in Corcovado National Park.*

ABOVE: *The armoured skin of the Nine-banded Armadillo (*Dasypus novemcinctus*) protects it from predators and tangled vegetation.*

gluey saliva that lubricates the anteater's tongue catches any insect it comes into contact with, and the tongue then whips the immobilized insects into the mouth. Anteaters have no teeth but do possess a muscular organ called a gizzard, which crushes the insects as they enter the digestive tract.

The time that an anteater spends at a single nest is very limited and usually doesn't last much longer than a few minutes. This is because the breach in the nest is soon swarming with soldier ants that run to defend their colony and attack the intruder with vicious bites from their huge, scissor-like jaws. Colonies of army ants and leaf-cutter ants have large numbers of soldiers and workers, and these can deliver a very painful bite. As a consequence, anteaters typically avoid these species of ant altogether.

Feeding on a nest for just a short time is actually advantageous for the anteater; by leaving the nest only partly damaged, the anteater ensures that the colony survives and it can return to feed on other occasions. When they are feeding on a nest, anteaters can consume hundreds of ants a minute. In one day they visit many different colonies from which they can eat thousands. The Giant Anteater can eat up to 30,000 insects in a single day. The Silky Anteater is too small to dig into large ant or termite nests. Instead, it breaks into hollow branches and stems that house colonies of these insects.

The claws of anteaters also provide them with an effective form of defence; in Costa Rica they are all preyed on by cats and the Silky Anteater is also eaten by birds of prey and even White-faced Capuchins. When threatened, all three species of anteater rear up onto their hind legs and lift their forelegs in the air. If a predator doesn't heed the warning growls or hisses, the anteater will thrash at the animal with its sharp claws, which will tear through flesh if the blows make contact. It is fairly common to hear stories from ex-hunters who had one of their dogs killed by a tamandua. The much larger Giant Anteaters can even defend themselves with their giant claws against Pumas and Jaguars.

Armadillos have much in common with anteaters. They feed on ants and termites and have elongated claws with which to break open their nests. Both the Nine-banded Armadillo and the Northern Naked-tailed Armadillo (*Cabassous centralis*) live in the forests of Costa Rica. They are usually active at night, when they amble through the undergrowth foraging for ant and termite nests, other insects and fruits.

The Nine-banded Armadillo has two very ingenious techniques for crossing bodies of water. If faced with a narrow stream it holds its breath and simply walks from one side to the other under the water. It can hold its breath for several minutes if necessary to achieve this. If the river is wider and deeper it ingests air into its intestines, which then provide it with enough buoyancy to float across on the surface of the water.

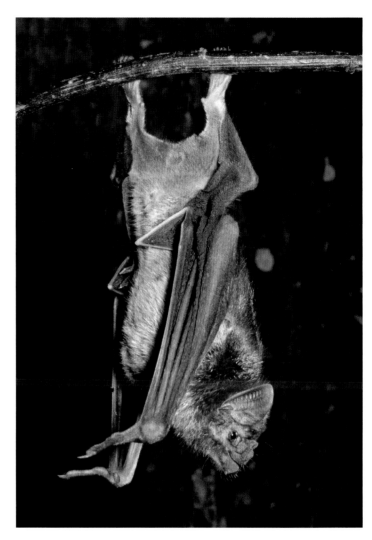

ABOVE: *The Bulldog Bat (*Noctilio leporinus*) uses echolocation to detect fish under the surface of the water.*

ABOVE, RIGHT: *The Common Vampire Bat (*Desmodus rotundus*) occasionally bites humans in Costa Rica.*

BATS

By far the largest group of mammals in Costa Rica is that of the bats. As many as 109 species have been recorded in the country and they constitute 12 per cent of all the bat species in the world. There are more bat species in Costa Rica than in the United States, Canada and Great Britain put together. This is very impressive if one considers that Costa Rica is roughly 380 times smaller than these three countries combined. Such a large number of similar animals is able to successfully co-inhabit a small country like Costa Rica for two reasons: firstly, because of their different feeding habits and secondly, because there is such an abundance of food.

Bats in Costa Rica feed on a wide range of animals and plants. Between them they eat other mammals (including other bats), birds, lizards, frogs, fish, insects, fruits, pollen, nectar and blood. Many species of bat have developed extremely specialized diets for which they have evolved both physical and physiological adaptations.

The Orange Nectar Bat (*Lonchophylla robusta*) feeds principally on the nectar and pollen of rainforest flowers that open at night. It has a pointed head that fits into the flower and a very long tongue with which to extract the nectar.

Both the Frog-eating Bat (*Trachops cirrhosus*) and the pug-nosed Bulldog Bat (*Noctilio leporinus*) hunt over water though they feed on very different prey. The Frog-eating Bat can precisely recognize the calls of the frogs that it eats and homes in on the source of the sound. The Bulldog Bat feeds on fish in freshwater canals and in the ocean close to the shore. It uses echolocation to detect the ripples that a fish creates when it is swimming just below the surface. Once the bat identifies its prey, it swoops down and snatches the fish from the water with large and powerful claws.

The Spectral Bat (*Vampyrum spectrum*) is the largest bat in Costa Rica and indeed, in all the Americas. It has an average wingspan of 80 cm though some individuals grow to as large as 1 m across. This bat is a fearsome predator with very large canine teeth and a powerful jaw, which it uses to catch its prey. It hunts in the rainforest, where it dives onto birds and lizards as they sleep on their night-time perches. It also seeks out small, nocturnal mammals that are active on the ground. The world's most famous bats are of course the vampire bats. There

are three species and all of them live in Costa Rica. The Common Vampire Bat (*Desmodus rotundus*) feeds mainly on the blood of livestock though it does very occasionally bite humans. It is common in the Guanacaste region of Costa Rica because of the large number of cattle ranches there. The White-winged Vampire Bat (*Diaemus youngi*) and the Hairy-legged Vampire Bat (*Diphylla ecaudata*) live in the forest, where they prey on sleeping birds.

Vampire bats feed by making a very small incision in their prey's skin and sucking up the blood that flows out. Their teeth are so sharp that the bite is usually not noticed by the sleeping animal. The bat's saliva contains an anticoagulant that prevents the blood from clotting and so allows the bat to continue feeding until its hunger is satisfied.

MONKEYS

The canopy of a tropical forest is a very rich source of food. Many mammals spend all their lives in the trees, where they can find young leaves, flowers, fruits, seeds, invertebrates and small vertebrates to feed on. Monkeys are the most commonly seen arboreal mammals in Costa Rica. They live in the dry forests, rainforests and cloud forests, as well as in some disturbed forests next to villages and farms. There are four very

ABOVE: *A female White-faced Capuchin (*Cebus capucinus) *carries her young in the canopy in Manuel Antonio National Park.*

different species found in the country. The White-faced Capuchin and the Mantled Howler Monkey are the two most frequently encountered. They inhabit both primary and secondary forest at all but the highest elevations and also disturbed areas of forest. The Spider Monkey is much less common and lives only in sizeable areas of pristine forest in the larger national parks. The distribution of the remaining species, the Squirrel Monkey, is even more limited, with only a few groups remaining on the south and central Pacific coast.

The White-faced Capuchin appears to be the most intelligent of the four species. It demonstrates this with its use of tools, something no other species of monkey in Costa Rica has been recorded doing. It uses twigs for extracting insects from holes and throws sticks at predators such as large snakes. White-faced Capuchins have also been observed hunting squirrels in groups in Costa Rica. This coordinated entrapment of prey between several individuals is better known from the primates of Africa and Asia.

Capuchins will combine their intelligence with a confidence that the other monkey species in Costa Rica don't man-

ABOVE: *A male Mantled Howler Monkey* (Alouatta palliata) *announces himself to neighbouring troops with a loud roar.*

have a varied diet of both plant material and small animals and so can find something that they can eat in almost every tree they visit. Despite the small size of their range, Capuchins are very active within this area and are almost permanently on the move.

The Mantled Howler Monkey is a complete contrast to the White-faced Capuchin. It is lethargic, passive and travels with its troop just a very short distance each day (its home range is less than 1 sq km). This behaviour is primarily a consequence of its diet, which is based heavily on leaves. The energy that the monkey obtains from eating even large quantities of leaves is extremely low, so it invests as little energy as possible in moving around. Howlers are most often encountered lying along tree branches, slowly digesting their cellulose-rich meals. They often do this in direct sunlight to gain valuable extra heat that accelerates the digestive process.

Because of their subsistence on commonly found food and their small home ranges, howler monkeys are able to venture out into disturbed forest more than any other species of monkey. They can often be seen in roadside trees and close to urban developments in the countryside.

Although it is one of the calmest animals in the forests of Costa Rica, the Mantled Howler

ifest. In Manuel Antonio National Park on the central Pacific coast, the capuchins have become so used to the presence of tourists that they show little worry as they steal unguarded food from the picnic tables next to the beach. Capuchins are also the most aggressive monkeys in Costa Rica, in particular the alpha male of a troop. They will sometimes chase other monkey species from a tree and shake or throw branches at humans on the ground. The home range of a White-faced Capuchin troop tends to be no more than 1.5 sq km. This is because they

Monkey is also the loudest. Males of different troops call to each other to announce their presence and avoid surprise encounters, which can lead to a confrontation that neither monkey benefits from. Their call is a deep, resounding roar that can carry for up to 1.5 km through the forest. To achieve this, they have a large chamber next to their vocal chords that amplifies the sounds they produce. Many visitors to Costa Rica have jumped out of their skin upon hearing this call for the very first time in the middle of the jungle.

At first glance, a Mantled Howler Monkey in the canopy can be confused with a Spider Monkey. They are similar in size, each growing to a body length of about 50 cm, and both

ABOVE: *The Spider Monkey (*Ateles geoffroyi*) has tiny vestigal thumbs so it can use its hands like hooks for gripping branches.*
RIGHT: *The Squirrel Monkey (*Saimiri oerstedii*) is a very active forager that travels in troops of up to 50 individuals.*

have long, dark fur with a reddish tinge. Spider Monkeys can be easily distinguished from Howlers, however, in the way they move. Spider Monkeys have long arms and legs and a fully prehensile tail that they use to swing effortlessly between trees. Their thumbs have evolved into tiny vestigial digits that are no longer visible. This allows the hands to act like hooks for grasping one branch after another, unhindered by the pres-

ABOVE: *The extremely rare Oncilla (*Leopardus tigrina*) lives in high-altitude forest and grows only slightly larger than a domestic cat.*

ence of a thumb. The reason why Spider Monkeys have developed such dexterity is that they feed predominantly on fruits that are only available on a seasonal basis. Therefore, they have to travel widely to constantly find enough fruiting trees to satisfy their needs. Their home ranges are usually several times larger than those of the leaf-eating Howler Monkey and the omnivorous Capuchin.

The smallest and least common species of monkey in Costa Rica is the Squirrel Monkey. These orange-coloured monkeys jump, climb and dive through the vegetation in troops of 20–50 individuals as they forage. They can flush out so many invertebrates when they travel that their troops are sometimes followed by foraging birds. The Tawny-winged Woodcreeper (*Dendrocincla anabatina*) and the Grey-headed Tanager (*Eucometis penicillata*) regularly follow army ants on the jungle floor, but have also been reported feeding in the midst of a troop of Squirrel Monkeys.

Squirrel Monkeys are now in danger of extinction in Costa Rica. Only a small population remains, with troops surviving in Manuel Antonio National Park, Corcovado National Park and fragments of forest in between. Their demise in recent years has been a result of habitat loss. Manuel Antonio National Park represents just 16 sq km of protected land that is now almost entirely isolated from other wild areas because of urban development, crop plantations and other farms around its boundaries. Corcovado has suffered a similar fate, although it provides a larger area of 480 sq km.

CATS

A hike through a gloomy rainforest, along an isolated beach or over a silent, treeless *paramo* becomes that little bit more exciting with the knowledge that you are in the territory of a wild cat. In Costa Rica felines roam through areas of wilderness from the seashore to the upper slopes of the highest mountains.

Wild cats are large carnivores that have very few or no natural predators in Costa Rica. They are thus grouped at the top end of the food chain, which means there are relatively few of them in comparison to the omnivores, herbivores and smaller carnivores further down the chain. They are also naturally wary of humans and as a result, tracks in the mud or sand are much more commonly seen than the animals themselves. In fourteen years of travelling and photographing in the parks and reserves of Costa Rica, I have never had close visual contact with any species of wild cat more than once. Wild cats have very well-developed senses of sight and hearing, which guide them to their prey in the thick tangle of forest undergrowth and even in the almost total darkness of night. They also have razor-sharp claws for grasping their prey, as well as large canine teeth and a powerful jaw to administer their killing bite. In Costa Rica the wild cats are solitary animals, except for females accompanied by their cubs.

The six species of wild cat in Costa Rica vary in body weight from just 2 kg to an impressive 80 kg. Due to the different size of each species, it inhabits a slightly different niche and feeds on a different variety of prey. Competition between species is therefore limited and this is why all six species have been able to inhabit the same region.

The two smallest wild cats in Costa Rica are the Oncilla (*Leopardus tigrina*) and the Margay (*Leopardus wiedii*). Both are slightly larger than a domestic cat and the Margay is the heavier of the two. They have the typical yellow and black spotted fur of forest cats that provides them with excellent camouflage. Very little is known of the Oncilla, although it is believed to have a similar natural history to that of the Margay, which applies its excellent climbing and jumping skills to hunting small mammals, birds, reptiles, frogs and insects in the trees. It

hunts mainly at night in undisturbed dry, rain and cloud forest throughout the country.

The medium-sized wild cats of Costa Rica are the Jaguarundi and the Ocelot. They have similar body lengths of between 65 and 90 cm plus tail, though the muscular Ocelot can grow to a weight of 15 kg – more than double that of the much slimmer Jaguarundi.

The Ocelot is yellow with black spots and can be distinguished from the Margay and Oncilla by its larger size. It hunts opportunistically on small mammals, lizards and birds on the forest floor and will sometimes climb trees, especially to sleep during the day. Its prey is usually much smaller than itself, but when the opportunity arises it will occasionally pounce on a more challenging opponent such as a large snake or even a caiman.

The Jaguarundi can have black, brown or grey fur and is the most frequently seen cat in Costa Rica. This is because it is probably the most common of the cat species and also because it is active during the day. An adult Jaguarundi differs from the

BELOW: *The Margay (*Leopardus wiedii*) is an expert climber and hunts animals from large insects to small mammals in trees at night.*

ABOVE: *The Ocelot (*Leopardus pardalis*) has exceptional night vision.*
RIGHT: *The powerful build of the Puma (*Puma concolor*) enables it to easily overwhelm prey like monkeys, anteaters and even deer.*

other cats in more than just its colour – its small face is weasel-like, and it has a long, thin body and an elongated tail. Its cubs are more cat-like at birth because they have spotted fur. The Jaguarundi has a similar diet to that of the Ocelot, although competition is minimal because they generally feed at different times of the day and the Jaguarundi will live in both virgin and disturbed forest, whereas the Ocelot seldom ventures out of undisturbed wildernesses.

The two largest land predators in Costa Rica are the Puma and the Jaguar. Between them these formidable predators will stalk and attack any other sizeable animal in the forest or on the beach, combining stealth and aggression to overcome their prey. Their favourite hunting technique is to creep up on an animal and then pounce on it. They use their huge clawed feet to control the prey while they deliver a powerful, lethal bite to its head or the back of its neck. Jaguars sometimes ambush their prey by dropping on top of it from a tree branch – the mottled colouration of their fur makes them hard to distinguish from the browns, greens and yellows of a sunlight-speckled forest. Jaguars and Pumas typically feed on medium-sized animals such as agoutis, iguanas, peccaries, armadillos, anteaters

and sloths, though they are perfectly able and willing to hunt larger animals. Pumas in Costa Rica are slightly smaller then those that live in North America, but still grow to over 1 m in body length and weigh approximately 50 kg. They will tackle ground prey as large as a peccary or even a deer, and are so agile that they can literally jump into a tree, where they snatch monkeys from the lower branches. A fully grown, 80 kg Jaguar will attack even bigger and more formidable animals such as Ocelots, Boa Constrictors, tapirs and sea turtles.

During the turtle-nesting seasons in Santa Rosa, Corcovado and Tortuguero National Parks, Jaguars hunt on the beach as well as in the forest. They kill adult turtles that come ashore at night to lay their eggs and then drag the 200 kg carcass across the sand and into the forest, where they hide it from other predators and return to feed on subsequent days. Their ability to pull such a weight 100 m or more, sometimes over logs and exposed roots, is evidence of the incredible strength of their jaws. Relative to its size, the Jaguar is reported to have the strongest bite of all cats. Lions and tigers are the only members of the cat family that grow larger and heavier than Jaguars.

Large cats such as Pumas and Jaguars require very big territories to find all the food they require. The areas in which they live must also be interconnected so that individuals from different regions can mate and therefore ensure a large, healthy breeding population. Pumas and Jaguars are now both seriously endangered in Costa Rica due to habitat destruction and

the hunting of both them and some of their preferred prey. Both these species are now extremely rare outside the country's largest protected areas, and unless new biological corridors are created between these regions the future survival of the populations that remain is extremely uncertain.

OLINGO AND KINKAJOU

The Kinkajou and the Olingo are two very similar-looking nocturnal mammals. The Kinkajou lives in all forest types throughout the country, while the Olingo prefers the cloud forest environment and rainforest on the Caribbean slope.

These two animals are strictly arboreal and scurry from branch to branch in search of fruits, flowers, nectar, insects and the occasional small vertebrate. Both species have very agile hands that enable them to climb and handle food with great dexterity. The Kinkajou has a very long tongue that it uses to extract nectar from deep within a flower, and a prehensile tail from which it can hang to reach food at the very end of a branch. The Olingo does not have a prehensile tail and this is the easiest way to distinguish between the two species.

At sunrise, Kinkajous and Olingos retire to the darkness and safety of a hollow tree, where they sleep through the day. Despite their cuddly appearance they can both deliver a nasty bite if disturbed in their den by a predator such as a cat. The Olingo and the Kinkajou belong to the family Procyonidae.

ABOVE: *The Kinkajou* (Potos flavus) *has a long, prehensile tail that it uses to grasp branches like a fifth limb.*

Other members of this family of omnivorous, medium-sized mammals that are common in Costa Rica are the Northern Raccoon, Crab-eating Raccoon and White-nosed Coati.

FRESHWATER MAMMALS

The rivers and natural canals that wind through the jungle in Costa Rica are home to several mammal species.

The West Indian Manatee (*Trichechus manatus*) is a huge animal that lives in the murky waters of the Caribbean lowland canals and lagoons. It is descended from the elephants and can reach a maximum size of 3 m in length and a weight of up to 500 kg. It has a large, flat tail-fin that it uses to swim slowly through the water as it grazes on floating plants and vegetation that hangs down from the canal bank. The manatee has a slow metabolism, meaning its body uses relatively little oxygen, which allows it to remain submerged for over fifteen minutes – one reason why these mammals are seldom seen. Sadly, there are now very few manatees left in Costa Rica. They were heavily hunted for their pelts until the 1980s and the contamination of their habitat by pesticides from nearby banana plantations has also accelerated their demise. Another danger is posed by the propellers of some motor boats that speed along the canals.

RIGHT: *A small number of West Indian Manatees* (Trichechus manatus) *survive in lowland Caribbean waterways.*
BELOW: *The Tucuxi (*Sotalia fluviatilis*) is a fresh-water dolphin that travels along rivers and canals.*

Sometimes the dorsal fin of a dolphin can be seen breaking the surface of the water in canals and rivers close to the Atlantic coast. The Tucuxi (*Sotalia fluviatilis*) is a species of dolphin that spends most of its life in fresh water, feeding on fish and crustaceans. In Costa Rica it is common in the River Sixaola on the Panamanian border, where it travels several kilometres upstream in search of food. Small numbers of individuals also inhabit other waterways further up the coast to Tortuguero National Park and Barra del Colorado Wildlife Refuge.

The Tucuxi is similar to the Bottlenose Dolphin, which also ventures into fresh water, but stays closer to the ocean.

Wild animals can be seen more easily if they are approached slowly and in silence. Travelling by canoe on Costa Rica's waterways is one way of doing this. One freshwater mammal in Costa Rica that will tolerate human presence if not startled is the Neotropical River Otter (*Lontra longicaudis*). It is found in rivers on both sides of the country, and is often seen in the canals of Tortuguero and Caño Negro. This species is an excellent swimmer that darts through the water to catch fish, crustaceans, frogs and even small birds. It often climbs from the water onto a rock or a fallen tree to eat the prey it catches and also to defecate, which is how males mark their territories. Neotropical River Otters sometimes travel in family

groups of a female with her young. Individuals chatter to each other as they forage and if one spots a predator, such as a caiman, it will alert the others with a high-pitched whistle.

A close relative of the Neotropical River Otter that also lives in Costa Rica is the rare Greater Grison (*Galictis vittata*). Both species belong to the weasel family Mustelidae and are physically similar, although the Greater Grison has a shorter tail and a grey and black coat unlike the reddish-brown and white fur of the otter. The grison is terrestrial and aquatic, with partially webbed feet to help it swim in the water. While foraging on land, the grison is very aggressive and will attack mammals its own size and large snakes.

OTHER MAMMALS

There are many other species and indeed, entire orders of mammal that inhabit the wildernesses of Costa Rica.

The dog family (Canidae) is represented by the Grey Fox (*Urocyon cinereoargenteus*) and the Coyote (*Canis latrans*), both of which hunt in the highlands and on the Pacific slope. Another medium-sized predator is the Tayra (*Eira barbara*). This black, cat-like mammal is actually a member of the weasel family with a long, bushy tail. It is quite common in forests except at the highest elevations, and feeds on a wide range of food like fruits, birds' eggs, venomous snakes and even monkeys and sloths.

ABOVE: *A Great Grison (*Galictis vittata*) carries its bird prey away to feed.*
OPPOSITE, ABOVE: *The Grey Fox (*Urocyon cinereoargenteus*) is primarily nocturnal, but can sometimes be seen during the day.*
OPPOSITE, BELOW: *The Tayra (*Eira barbara*) has a powerful bite that can quickly kill prey such as venomous snakes.*

There are many rodent species in Costa Rica. The Central American Agouti (*Dasyprocta punctata*) is a common, ground-dwelling omnivore that roams through the forest understory shadows during the day gnawing on fallen seeds and fruits. The Paca (*Agouti paca*) is a similar, larger rodent active only at night. It weighs about 8 kg when fully grown and is a favourite prey of the larger cats.

White-tailed Deer (*Odocoileus virginianus*) are extremely common in the protected dry forests of Guanacaste, and the slightly smaller Red Brocket Deer (*Mazama americana*) inhabits rainforest and cloud forest in many areas.

Eight species of terrestrial and arboreal opossum have been recorded in Costa Rica. Possibly the most curious is the Water Opossum (*Chironectes minimus*) – the only marsupial that hunts underwater. It has webbed hind feet and a long tail that propel it through the water of streams and lakes in pursuit of fish, frogs and crustaceans, which it catches with its forefeet.

CHAPTER 3
VOLCANOES OF COSTA RICA

Among the cloud-covered peaks of Costa Rica's mountain ranges there are gaping holes in the rock where the Earth's burning interior escapes to the surface. Explosions of bright red molten rock, super-heated pyroclastic flows, smouldering craters, brightly coloured lakes of acid, bubbling mud pools and earth tremors are everyday occurrences on this section of the Pacific Ring of Fire, which stretches from South America round to Australasia.

LEFT: *The lagoon in the 1.3 km-wide crater of Poás Volcano is highly acidic and can reach temperatures of up to 50°C.*

A BACKBONE OF MOUNTAINS

There are over 100 volcanic craters in Costa Rica that have erupted at some time in the country's past. The reason why Costa Rica has so many volcanoes is that it lies at the junction of two tectonic plates in the Earth's crust. The Cocos and Caribbean plates meet far underneath the country's Pacific coast, where their interaction creates ruptures in the Earth's surface through which gases and molten rock escape. Prolonged activity of this kind creates volcanoes.

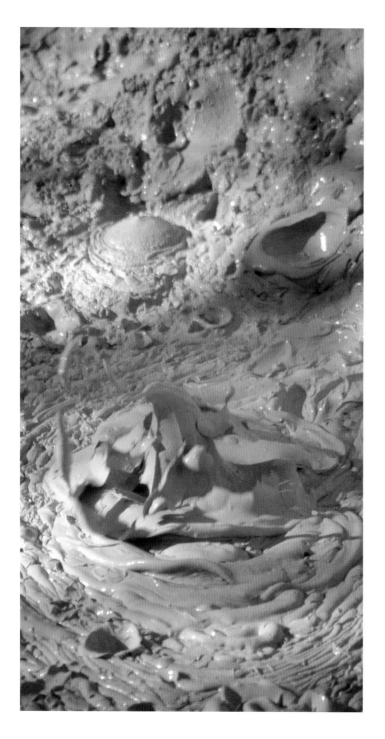

The craters comprise an integral part of the backbone of mountains that runs down the centre of Costa Rica. The most recognized of these volcanoes are, in order from the north-west to the south-east: Orosí, Rincón de la Vieja, Miravalles, Tenorio, Arenal, Poás, Barva, Irazú and Turrialba. Neither Orosí nor Barva Volcanoes have shown activity for several thousand years and are dormant or extinct. All of the other seven are considered active. The Miravalles Volcano manifests secondary volcanic activity (hot mud and water springs), and this energy is harnessed by a geothermic power station run by the Costa Rican Electricity Board. There are fumaroles at Tenorio Volcano and Turrialba Volcano, and strong eruptions have been produced from Rincón de la Vieja, Arenal, Poás and Irazú in the last fifteen years.

RINCÓN DE LA VIEJA VOLCANO

Nine craters lie embedded in the mountain top that overlooks Rincón de la Vieja National Park. They are part of a ridge-shaped massif that covers 400 sq km and is estimated to be half a million years old. The three most prominent craters are positioned in a line that runs north-west to south-east. The most north-westerly is the dormant Von Seebach crater, which sits at an altitude of 1,895 m. A spectacular view of lowlands to the west greets intrepid walkers who reach this summit, as well as a battering from the winds that race over the Guanacaste Cordillera. A corrugated slope of old lava flows leads down from here to the active Rincón de la Vieja crater next to it; this has almost vertical internal walls that plunge down more than 100 m to an acidic lake below. The colour of this lake periodically changes between sky-blue and light grey. Written records that detail violent eruptions from this crater date back to the middle of the 18th century. As recently as the 1980s and '90s, several eruptions shook the mountain, including one in February 1983 that cast rocks 1 km down the southern slope. Since 1998 only fumarolic activity has been observed, and hik-

LEFT: *Sulphurous gases escape through a pool of boiling mud in Rincón de la Vieja National Park.*

ers are allowed to walk up to the edge of the crater. To the south-east of the active crater, a cloud forest swathes the highest of the three peaks – the dormant Santa María crater. Within the national park, to the south of Rincón de la Vieja Volcano, is a series of boiling mud pools and thermal springs. The hot, sulphurous gases that cause them rise through vents in the earth from pools of lava deep below this volcanic landscape.

ARENAL VOLCANO

For at least 500 years, Arenal Volcano had remained inactive and quiet. 'Arenal Hill', as it was known to locals, was a modestly sized, 1,400 m-tall, cone-shaped mound covered in thick

ABOVE: *A cloud of hot ash rises from the crater of Arenal Volcano following a small eruption.*

primary rainforest that extended down into the crater at its peak. Agricultural communities had established themselves at its base and hunters spent nights in this depression, safely enjoying the heat provided to them by the curiously warm boulders. The years of tranquillity ended abruptly on the evening of 28 July 1968, when local residents were kept awake by unusually strong and repeated earth tremors. The following morning at 7.30 a.m., a massive eruption burst from the hillside. Pyroclastic flows of super-heated gases raced down the slope, vaporizing vegetation over an area of 12 sq km and destroying the villages of Tabacón and Pueblo Nuevo. Huge rocks from the explosion were later discovered 5 km from the mountain, half buried in 20 m-wide impact craters. Eighty-seven people lost their lives to the awakening of Arenal Volcano, in what remains one the most tragic natural disasters ever recorded in Costa Rica.

The eruption created three new craters on the western flank of the volcano, the most active of which was formed halfway down the hillside. Two months later, lava was seen flowing from this point for the first time.

Since 1968 Arenal Volcano has been constantly active, producing lava, ash and gas on a daily basis. The mountain stands 1,633 m above sea level and looms 1,383 m above the town of La Fortuna. This is almost 200 m taller than it was in 1968, which is a result of the accumulation of layer upon layer of debris from the numerous eruptions. The volcano presently has two similarly sized peaks, each with its own smouldering crater. The slightly taller north-west crater is the source of lava flows, avalanches and eruptions, while the other peak demonstrates only fumarolic activity.

The first sign of an eruption is a plume of grey smoke that billows from the volcano's crater and can sometimes reach a height of more than 1 km. There is a short delay before a thunderous boom can be heard; when observed from 1 km away, the sound of an eruption takes three seconds to reach your ears. The rising cloud of hot gases, ash and lava fragments fans out as it is blown westwards by the wind towards Lake Arenal. Sizeable eruption clouds drop fine pellets of ash on the ground below several minutes later.

A common result of many of the eruptions from Arenal Volcano is a pyroclastic flow. These mixtures of hot gas, rocks and ash travel down the flank of the volcano at speeds of up to 120 km an hour and can continue for 1 km. They are the most dangerous aspect of the volcano's current activity. The city of Pompeii in Italy was famously destroyed in AD 79 by pyroclastic flows. During one of my photography trips to Arenal, a huge pyroclastic flow created an enormous, dense cloud of ash that engulfed all of the land and water between the volcano and the park ranger station to the west. Some of the park staff and I took refuge in the visitors' centre just as the curtain of ash enveloped the building. Though the ash was no longer hot, it served as a reminder of the power that the volcano has.

Arenal Volcano is most impressive at night, when streams of red lava can be seen snaking down from the summit. This lava can be as hot as 1,200°C when it appears from the cone; as it flows over the ground it gradually cools and becomes solid rock. The flanks of the volcano are ribbed by a series of old lava flows.

When the volcano erupts, each red-hot projectile casts a thin red line that arcs through the sky like those of an explod-

ing firework. Through binoculars or a powerful telephoto lens individual boulders, some larger than a car, can be seen bouncing and crashing down the mountainside.

A stone's throw to the south of Arenal Volcano is Cerro Chato, another, smaller mountain that was also an active volcano many years ago. Its extinct crater is filled with rainwater and enveloped by lush rainforest. From its edge, at an altitude of 1,140 m, Arenal Volcano can be seen from the side rather than the usual view of from below. Looked at in this way, the active volcano appears to be a lot closer than it really is.

Arenal Volcano National Park protects 121 sq km of countryside around the volcano. Rainforest grows on its eastern and southern slopes and extends southwards over Cerro Chato, where it eventually merges with the Monteverde Cloud Forest Preserve and the Children's Eternal Rainforest in the Tilarán Mountain Range. Birdlife is rich in the park and populations of

ABOVE: *Boulders mark the site of a giant lava flow that ran down Arenal Volcano in 1992, obliterating a large area of rainforest.*

larger mammals such as the Mantled Howler Monkey, White-faced Capuchin and Collared Peccary are well established in the forest.

There are few trees at the foot of the western slope of the volcano because of the fallout of ash that consistently showers the area. Grasses and shrubs dominate this semi-barren land-scape, which is brightened by the commonly encountered red and yellow terrestrial orchid *Epidendrum radicans*.

POÁS VOLCANO

The sheer size of Poás Volcano takes onlookers several seconds to assimilate. From the viewpoint at the very lip of the crater one can gaze across the gigantic caldera to its opposite slope an incredible 1.3 km away. This makes it one of the widest active volcanic craters in the world. In the centre of this enormous hole is a 300 m-wide lake of bubbling acid, the pH of which never rises above 1.5, while the temperature can reach 50°C. Changes in the activity of the volcano cause changes in the colour of this lagoon. Some months the surface is bright blue, sometimes it is green, and during others it is a nondescript grey.

The regular fumarolic activity of Poás Volcano is controlled by a body of molten rock that sits hundreds of metres below the crater. This magma maintains a temperature of 800 to 1,200°C and produces super-hot gases of sulphur dioxide, hydrogen sulphide and hydrogen chloride that rise to the Earth's surface. Sometimes these gases escape directly into the atmosphere through fumarole vents in the crater walls, shooting hundreds of metres into the air. They are then carried by the wind across the landscape, and severely damage forest and crops when they accumulate in sufficiently high concentrations. At other times, the gases are released into the bottom of the 40 m-deep crater lagoon, where they mix with water. The most toxic product of this reaction is hydrochloric acid, which is responsible for the extremely high acidity of the lake. During periods of heightened underground volcanic activity, the temperature of the lagoon rises and the hydrochloric acid evaporates into the air as hydrogen chloride gas. These clouds of acidic gas are the cause of acid rain that falls on the surrounding countryside up to 15 km away. The resulting damage can be clearly seen downwind of the volcano on its south-west slope, where the terrain is devoid of vegetation. Sometimes the local inhabitants are also affected directly by this toxic fallout.

Poás Volcano has been visibly active for at least the last 260 years. Large eruptions occurred in 1834 and 1910, when the discharged ash fell across a large area of the central valley. The eruption of 1910 produced a mushroom cloud that was estimated to be about 8 km high; the ash fell as far away as Cartago. There was also intense activity in 1953, 1961 and 1963 that involved powerful eruptions. Despite these alarming events, local people still visited the crater of the volcano, sometimes to collect liquid from the lagoon, which they used for medicinal purposes. Indigenous tribes are believed to have done the same in previous times.

The Poás Volcano National Park was created in 1970 and from then onwards access to the lagoon of the active crater was prohibited for safety reasons. This was a wise decision considering that the gases escaping from the volcano's fumaroles sometimes reach temperatures of almost 1,000°C.

The most recent eruptions occurred in 1989, 1994 and 2006. A series of eruptions in September 2006 was relatively small but significant, throwing water and sediment 360 m up into the air and chunks of sulphur and rock several hundred metres across the crater floor.

Poás Volcano rises 2,700 m above sea level and is clearly visible from San José, 45 km to the south-east. The air is chilly at this altitude, and strong winds race across the mountainous divide. By mid-morning, clouds begin to roll over the lip of the crater and intermittently hide the colossal structure from view. Cloud forest cloaks the north, east and south slopes, where dense populations of the Poor Man's Umbrella (*Gunnera insignis*) thrive on the acidic soil. Some eye-catching flowers grow near the summit; the bright pink Melastoma of the Volcanoes (*Monochaetum vulcanicum*) is prevalent up to the very lip of the crater all the year round, and the bright yellow Common Gorse (*Ulex europaeus*) lines the park trails. When it is in flower, the highland bromeliad *Werauhia ororiensis* produces a magnificent red and yellow inflorescence that can grow to

RIGHT: *Lush cloud forest vegetation encloses Botos Lagoon in Poás Volcano National Park.*

ABOVE: *The bright flowers of the bromeliad* Werauhia ororiensis *attract hummingbirds, which pollinate the flowers as they feed.*
LEFT: *The Melastoma of the Volcanoes (*Monochaetum vulcanicum*) and Common Gorse (*Ulex europaeus*) at the crater of Poás Volcano.*
OPPOSITE: *The enormous leaves of the Poor Man's Umbrella (*Gunnera insignis*) grow to more than a metre across.*

an impressive height of 75 cm. This explosion of colour attracts the Magnificent Hummingbird (*Eugenes fulgens*) to feed.

Just 800 m from the main crater lies the picturesque Botos Lagoon. This 9 m-deep, freshwater lake fills another volcanic crater that is now extinct. Between the two sites grows a moss-covered elfin cloud forest that provides welcome shelter from the cold winds.

Birds such as the orange-breasted Flame-throated Warbler (*Parula gutturalis*) and the bright yellow Collared Redstart (*Myioborus torquatus*) probe the moss and lichen for hidden insects, and the splendid Emerald Toucanet also inhabits this forest. The Poás Squirrel (*Syntheosciurus brochus*) is very common near the Botos Lagoon, although its only other official sighting in the whole country has been in Tapantí National Park. Outside Costa Rica it has been reported in the Chiriquí highlands of Panama and, interestingly, nowhere else.

BARVA VOLCANO

The 2,906 m-high Barva Volcano lies within the western boundary of Braulio Carrillo National Park. Its summit looks down on the town of Heredia, and pastures and coffee plantations cover its lower slopes. It differs structurally from all the other volcanoes in Costa Rica in that it is a complex of numerous ancient craters spread out across three main peaks, known locally as 'The Three Marías'. At least twelve volcanic cones have been identified under the cloud forest covering the top of this enormous mountain. The volcano is most commonly identified with the Barva Lagoon, which fills the youngest of these forest-lined craters. The Resplendent Quetzal and many other cloud-forest animals live in this quiet and undisturbed habitat.

The last big eruption at Barva occurred approximately 6,000 years ago. There were reports of eruptions in the 18th and 19th centuries, although there is some dispute as to whether the events were the cause of volcanic activity or not. At present, Barva Volcano is classed as dormant and shows no signs of fumaroles or the release of gases.

IRAZÚ VOLCANO

The tallest volcano in Costa Rica is Irazú. At 3,432 m above sea level it is also one of the country's highest peaks, which is surpassed only by a handful of mountains in the Talamanca mountain range.

Sparse vegetation grows on the barren landscape around the active, 1 km-wide main crater and the smaller Diego de la Haya crater next to it. The enormous-leafed Poor Man's Umbrella is the most common plant that roots in the rocky, ash-covered ground, and Indian's paintbrush (*Castilleja* spp.) flowers provide occasional splashes of red to the panorama.

The walls of the main crater slope steeply down by almost 200 m to a pool of greenish-yellow water, the colour of which is due to the algae that float on its surface. This small lagoon is formed by rainwater, which is currently replaced at the same rate as it seeps down into the mountain. Between the late 1960s and late '80s, however, the water filtered out of the crater much faster than it does now, so visitors would only see a lagoon during periods of heavy rainfall. The water in the crater of Irazú is slightly acidic and has an average temperature of 15°C, although hot gases heat some areas to 40°C at some times.

Written records of Irazú Volcano's activity date back to the year 1723. In recent times, a series of strong eruptions between 1963 and 1965 covered large areas of San José, Heredia and Alajuela in ash, and caused mud slides that

ABOVE: *Indian's paintbrush flowers (Castilleja sp.) are one of the few plants to survive the cold and wind at Irazú Volcano's summit.*
OPPOSITE: *Floating algae are responsible for the bright green colour of the rainwater lake inside Irazú Volcano's crater.*

claimed a number of human lives on the volcano's southern slope above the city of Cartago. The last sizeable eruption took place in 1994, when avalanches of rocks travelled 20 km along the course of the Río Sucio on the northern flank of the volcano.

Presently, the only activity from inside the main crater of Irazú Volcano is the release of small amounts of hot gases.

TURRIALBA VOLCANO

Turrialba Volcano offers the very rare opportunity to actually walk inside an active volcanic crater. Its vast, rocky caldera, which peaks at 3,340 m, is over 2 km in length and contains three separate craters.

The most westerly crater is the centre of activity, with hot, toxic gases and steam escaping from fumaroles in its walls. From inside the adjacent, central crater, these emissions can be clearly seen and the smell of sulphur lingers in the air. Shallow, light-blue lagoons of acidic water temporarily appear

in both this and a third, small, eastern crater after periods of heavy rainfall.

Turrialba Volcano is just 12 km to the north-east of Irazú Volcano and is 16 km from the centre of the town of Turrialba. It has experienced at least five periods of powerful eruptions over the last 3,500 years. The most recent was in the 19th century, ending in 1866 with an explosion of such force that it threw ash as far away as Nicaragua. Hot, toxic gases and steam have been rising from the depths of Turrialba ever since. In early 2007 the level of activity began to rise significantly once again, destroying long tracts of vegetation on the downwind, western slope. Columns of escaping gas could be seen above the lip of the crater by local villagers, and the park was consequently closed to visitors as a safety precaution.

Irazú and Turrialba Volcanoes represent a serious potential threat to the capital San José and the surrounding populations. Both are very tall, large and active volcanoes that lie upwind of the Central Valley. The ash produced during a large eruption from either of them could severely disrupt many thousands of households, businesses and the transportation system. The international airport in Alajuela could also be rendered inoperative. A more serious scenario would also involve the loss of many lives.

CHAPTER 4

THE SUMMIT OF COSTA RICA – MOUNT CHIRRIPÓ

Almost 4 km above the palm-shaded beaches and hot, steamy jungles of the Costa Rican lowlands there is a sharp, rocky summit where no trees grow and icicles form at night. With a view of two oceans and looking down on the clouds, this mountain is the pinnacle of the Talamanca Mountain Range. At 3,819 m above sea level, Mount Chirripó is taller than any other mountain in neighbouring Panama, Nicaragua, El Salvador and Honduras. To hike from its lower slopes to the peak is a unique journey through rainforest, cloud forest and subalpine paramo. *The changes in vegetation, wildlife and climate are dramatic, and at the very end of the trail the views are witnessed in an awed silence.*

LEFT: *Hikers look down on Las Morenas Valley from the summit of Mount Chirripó.*

COSTA RICA'S HIGHEST MOUNTAIN

The Talamanca Range is the most southern of four mountain ranges that run end to end along the length of Costa Rica. It begins just south of the capital, San José, and extends down into the Chiriquí highlands of neighbouring Panama. This rugged wilderness boasts the highest non-volcanic peaks in the whole of Central America.

During the last Ice Age the Chirripó Massif was a frozen landscape of enormous glaciers and isolated rocky peaks. The gradual, downhill movement of these glaciers and the rocks that they dragged with them tore away the mountainsides, creating vast, U-shaped valleys and sharp mountain tops. When the Ice Age came to an end approximately 10,000 years ago, temperatures rose and the glaciers slowly began to melt and retreat. The rock debris and sand carried by glaciers was released from the melted ice and dumped within the carved valleys surrounding Mount Chirripó. This material enclosed ice-dug hollows in the valley floors, which collected melt water and later formed lakes. This debris is called moraine, hence the name of Las Morenas Valley at the base of Mount Chirripó, which has a cluster of sapphire-blue lakes scattered across its floor. It was perhaps the discovery of these stunningly beautiful lagoons that led local indigenous tribes to name this area around the country's tallest mountain the 'Land of Eternal Waters'.

In 1904, long after the mountain's name had been chosen by the locals, a local missionary called Agustín Blessing became the first person to officially record an ascent to the summit of Mount Chirripó. In the years that have followed, other religious figures, botanists, geologists and now tourists have risen to the challenge of exploring Costa Rica's highest mountain. The first official hiking trail was constructed in 1965, which led to a small, sheet-metal hut that was assembled in a valley 5 km from the summit. In 1975 the Chirripó National Park was founded, and within a few years the park's limits had expanded to enclose an impressive 500 sq km of rainforest, cloud forest and *paramo*. There is now a modern, concrete refuge where the first rustic hut once stood that is visited by around 7,000 national and foreign visitors every year.

The trek to the heights of Chirripó National Park traditionally begins just before daybreak in the tranquil village of San Gerardo, nestled 1,500 m above sea level in a small valley in the Talamanca Range. The steep, winding trail quickly accelerates one's heartbeat as it rises through fields of pasture and fragmented woodland before entering the shadows of lush montane rainforest. Dense vegetation sprawls across the

RIGHT: *Lake Chirripó lies on the subalpine* paramo *just a few hundred metres below the summit of Mount Chirripó.*

ground and buttress-rooted trees stretch up to form a single, continuous canopy of intermingled branches.

Suddenly there are new sounds to be heard. High up in the treetops the rustling of leaves reveals the presence of a troop of Spider Monkeys foraging for their first fruit of the day; the rhythmic tapping sound of a woodpecker floats through the cool air and a sudden warning shriek from the undergrowth alerts one to the presence of a family of ground-dwelling quail. Butterflies dance in the morning's first rays of sunshine, while tanagers, warblers and finches hop and flutter their way through the vegetation in search of insects and berries. From time to time the trail turns downwards, which provides a welcome relief to the lungs and thigh muscles. However, the reprieve is short-lived as the ground once again slopes steeply upwards and you are rudely reminded that the mountain has not yet been conquered.

After several hard-fought kilometres the park limit is reached at an elevation of 2,000 m. From here onwards the views through the trees are more of dense canopy and mountain peaks rather than distant farmland. The vegetation is that

ABOVE: 'Old Man's Beard' (Tillandsia *spp.) moss grows prolifically in the cloud forest of Chirripó National Park.*
OPPOSITE, ABOVE: *Possibly the most recognizable landmark in Chirripó National Park is the Los Crestones rock formation.*
OPPOSITE, BELOW: *In recent decades, fires have raged through large areas of cloud forest within sight of Los Crestones.*

of a Talamanca cloud forest; enormous oak trees with gnarled trunks and twisting branches tower up to 40 m above the trail, their limbs adorned with bright red bromeliads and carpets of hanging yellow-brown moss known locally as 'Old Man's Beard' (*Tillandsia* spp.). In the understorey, long stems of green bamboo curve through the air in search of the best light. Clouds regularly drift through this landscape, giving the forest an enchanted, even prehistoric appearance.

Though dozens of mammal and reptile species inhabit the high-elevation cloud forests between 2,000 and 3,200 m, by far the easiest animals to spot are birds. The laboured swooping of large wings will reveal the presence of a Black Guan (*Chamaepetes unicolor*) as it flies clumsily between perches. A flash of metallic green is the first, and sometimes the last that hikers will see of a Resplendent Quetzal, and the eerie 'squeaky gate' call of a Three-wattled Bellbird can travel from deep within the canopy. Flowers along the trail are magnets for hummingbirds including the Green Violet-ear (*Colibri thalassinus*) and the Grey-tailed Mountaingem (*Lampornis cinereicauda*). The gentle hum of their wings is often heard before they hover into view.

When the trail attains 3,200 m in elevation the cloud-forest canopy abruptly ends, birdsong is replaced with the sound of the wind and a radically different terrain lies ahead. Five major fires have swept across this area of Chirripó National Park since 1953, destroying hundreds of hectares of primary forest. What remains of the original vegetation are thousands of burnt and sun-bleached tree trunks that jut out of the mountainside like gravestones in a cemetery.

Wildlife is scarce here, although shrubs, ferns and small trees have begun the regeneration process and there are now many flowering plants that provide excellent opportunities to watch hummingbirds. The most common species along the trail is the Volcano Hummingbird (*Selasphorus flammula*), which lives in open habitats such as *paramo* and areas of regeneration created by fire. It is a small bird that measures about 8 cm in length and weighs on average a mere 2.5 g. Because of their small size females, and sometimes also males, feed on a variety of flowers over a relatively large area instead of trying to defend a localized territory from other, larger species of hummingbird.

ABOVE: *The well-insulated Sooty Robin (*Turdus nigrescens*) is one of the few birds that live on the* paramo.

The rocky trail that traverses this belt of semi-barren land ascends and descends the contours of several steep hills. From the crest of each, a short, jagged ridge of gigantic rocks called Los Crestones can be seen in the near distance. This ancient landmark sits above a bare and windswept subalpine *paramo*, which is the last life zone one enters on route to the summit of Chirripó. Facing Los Crestones across a small valley of grasses and shrubs is the day's final destination: the visitors' refuge.

The climate on the *paramo* of Chirripó is much more varied and unpredictable than at lower altitudes below the timberline. The temperature typically ranges from 4 to 15°C during any 24-hour period, though occasionally at night the thermometer reading will drop to several degrees below zero. At such times, at sunrise the frosted ground will crunch underfoot and dripping icicles can be seen hanging from the vegetation.

During the driest months of January to March, one has a very good chance of exploring Chirripó National Park under blue skies and sunshine. Nights are often cloudless, with thousands of stars twinkling between one horizon and another that feel just that little bit closer than normal. Seven months later in the middle of the wet season, visitors are likely to encounter a very different environment, with misty forests, rolling fog banks and regular rainfall.

In order to survive large temperature fluctuations, the drying effects of strong winds and periods of very little rainfall, plants on the *paramo* have developed special adaptations. Their leaves are small with thick cuticles to help reduce the rate at which they lose water by evaporation, which is accelerated by heat and wind. It also makes them hardier against the formation of frost and the sudden temperature rise associated with its melting on a sunny morning. Plants on the *paramo* are also relatively short. The tallest species that grows on the Chirripó massif is a dwarf bamboo that reaches little more than head height. By growing closer to the ground and in a more compact form, a plant is less exposed to the wind and cold.

A number of animals are also able to live under the harsh conditions that these altitudes present. Incredibly, two of the most commonly encountered species are cold-blooded. The Green Spiny Lizard (*Sceloporus malachiticus*) and the Highland Alligator Lizard (*Mesaspis monticola*) can be found throughout the *paramo* and even up to the very base of the peak of Mount Chirripó, 3,500 m above sea level. At these heights their lives depend on them being able to absorb and store as much heat as possible from the sun's rays. On a sunny day these reptiles will bask on rocks, flattening their bodies out to increase their surface area. Their non-shiny skin helps to keep the amount of reflected light to a minimum. At night, and when clouds block out the sun during the day, they seek refuge in tight crevices under stones where their heat can be more easily retained.

Unlike most reptiles, the Green Spiny Lizard and the Highland Alligator Lizard cannot lay eggs externally because the radical temperature changes and cold on these mountain tops would kill them. Instead, females of both species are ovoviviparous, which means the females keep their eggs inside the body until they hatch, bearing live young. By regulating her own body temperature, the female lizard is in turn doing the same for her eggs.

While hiking over the *paramo* one is struck by the lack of sounds. Indeed, when the wind drops to a perfect calm the landscape can become completely silent. One reason for this of course is the almost total absence of birds. The sparse vegetation and food resources provide little interest for most species, though there are some birds that have carved out a niche for themselves in these quiet valleys.

The Sooty Robin (*Turdus nigrescens*) and Volcano Junco (*Junco vulcani*) are birds that spend most of their time hopping along the ground and among shrubs in search of insects, berries and seeds. Both of these birds are common in the highlands of the Talamanca Mountain Range, and the Volcano Junco is a frequent visitor to the very summit of Chirripó, where it searches the rocks for crumbs dropped by snacking tourists.

Other birds have remained in the sky and have taken full advantage of the open spaces and clear views above the timberline. Swifts break the silence as they race past at high speed, creating a ripping sound in the air. In contrast to the Sooty Robin and Volcano Junco, these birds rarely land to feed because they snatch insects in flight.

The main predator and undisputed ruler of the *paramo* skies is the Red-tailed Hawk (*Buteo jamaicensis*), which soars across the landscape searching the ground with its sharp eyes for signs of small animals out in the open. When it spots a potential meal such as a rabbit, rodent, lizard or even a small bird, the hawk will hover, positioning itself against the wind, and then dive down onto its unsuspecting prey.

From high above the ground the Red-tailed Hawk will occasionally note the movement on the *paramo* of large mammals that it will regard with just a passing interest. The biggest of these is the Baird`s Tapir, which roams the *paramo* feeding

ABOVE: *A Volcano Hummingbird (*Selasphorus flammula*) feeds at a* Bomarea hirsuta *lily in fire-damaged growth bordering the* paramo. BELOW: *A Green Spiny Lizard (*Sceloporus malachiticus*) warms its body in the sun on the edge of Lake Chirripó.*

ABOVE: *The Veintisquineros mountain ridge looms above the cloud forest trail that leads to the visitors' refuge.*

on the abundance of herbs that grow there such as the locally named Arracachillo (*Myrrhidendron chirripoense*). Though tapirs are not common here, signs of their passing can sometimes be seen in the mud around Lakes Chirripó and Las Morenas. The tapir's huge, three-toed footprints are difficult to confuse with those of any other animal.

The other two sizeable mammals that live above the tree-line in Chirripó are the Puma and the Coyote. The Puma is very rarely seen because of its scarcity, stealth and tan-coloured fur that camouflages it so well on the *paramo*. It is very common, however, to come across its faeces on the trail that leads from the shelter to the summit of Mount Chirripó. Here it feeds

mainly on the resident Dice's Cottontail Rabbits (*Sylvilagus dicei*), which it stalks and pounces on with a speed that can match that of the fleeing rabbit. The Coyote is a long-eared, slender-legged and bushy-tailed version of the domestic dog that belongs to the Canidae family, which also includes foxes and wolves. It lives solitarily or in small groups, and because it is primarily nocturnal it can more commonly be heard rather than seen; in Chirripó its long, whining howl can carry for several kilometres across the open *paramo*. Coyotes burrow dens in the ground, which helps them to tolerate the cold, cloudy days in the highlands and shades them from the sun when the sky is clear. Like the Puma, Coyotes hunt rabbits on the *paramo*, but will also eat berries and even grass.

To reach the summit of Mount Chirripó from the refuge there remains a two-hour hike across the *paramo* and over one last

ridge. In order to be there for sunrise, the walk must begin at 3.30 a.m. in darkness.

The air is cold and the valley looks even more devoid of life and landmarks than during the day. Nevertheless, the hike is an exciting one because the race is now on to reach Costa Rica's highest point before the sun's rays do.

The trail rises and falls as it heads east across El Valle de Los Conejos ('Valley of the Rabbits'). Several invisible streams trickle past on the beginning of their long journey down to the ocean. The path eventually leads up out of the valley and over the final ridge. As the horizon ahead begins to lighten, a silhouette of the remaining 200 m of mountain is all that stands between the walking trail and space. The wind that drives across this bleak outcrop at these early hours numbs all feeling from exposed fingers and challenges even the sturdiest of tripods. Both hands and

ABOVE: *The trail climbs steeply before it reaches the summit of Mount Chirripó.*

feet are needed to scramble over the last few boulders, and then quite suddenly there is nothing else to climb.

The summit of Mount Chirripó is a 6 m-wide platform of rocks circled by a crown of grasses and shrubs. A red, white and blue flag flutters violently at the end of its pole in the centre.

The emerging sun illuminates seemingly endless files of mountain peaks that stretch away to the far north and south of the country. Down in the surrounding valleys an array of dark blue lakes is slowly unveiled by the retreating shadows. On a cloudless day both of the Pacific and Caribbean coastlines can be seen through the haze from here, the summit of Mount Chirripó.

CHAPTER 5

THE NATIONAL PARKS, REFUGES & RESERVES OF COSTA RICA

Since 1945, Costa Rica has built up a system of almost 250 national parks, wildlife refuges and biological reserves that cover roughly 20 per cent of its land area. The vast majority of this land is government-owned, although almost 150 private properties also account for a valuable part of the country's wildernesses.

LEFT: *The natural beauty of Costa Rica's Manuel Antonio National Park is breathtaking.*

PAST & FUTURE OF A FRAGILE NETWORK

Some of Costa Rica's protected areas, such as Poás Volcano and Manuel Antonio, are high-profile tourist destinations that receive over 200,000 sightseers per year, while others, such as Guanacaste and La Amistad National Parks, lie almost undisturbed with fewer than 100 human visitors each year.

The first wilderness area in Costa Rica to be declared a protected zone was an oak forest along the Pan American highway south of the city of Cartago in 1945. Ten years later, the land around the craters of some of Costa Rica's volcanoes was also placed under the protection of the government, which led to the formal inauguration of the country's first national parks on Turrialba and Irazú Volcanoes in July and August of 1955 respectively. Eight years later, the Cabo Blanco Absolute Nature Reserve was created on the Nicoya Peninsula. This was a result of the campaigning by local landowners Nicolás Wessberg and Karen Mogensen, who were appalled by the fast

rate of deforestation in the area. The first official government office dedicated to the creation, administration and protection of national parks was opened in 1969. The status and size of this office gradually grew throughout the 1970s and '80s until in 1998 it became the National System of Conservation Areas (SINAC) – this remains its name today.

The majority of the protected areas in Costa Rica were created individually between the 1970s and '90s. Each was established as a result of the desire to conserve the land and wildlife in the area. In 1971, the Santa Rosa National Park was created around a 19th-century hacienda known as 'La Casona', which

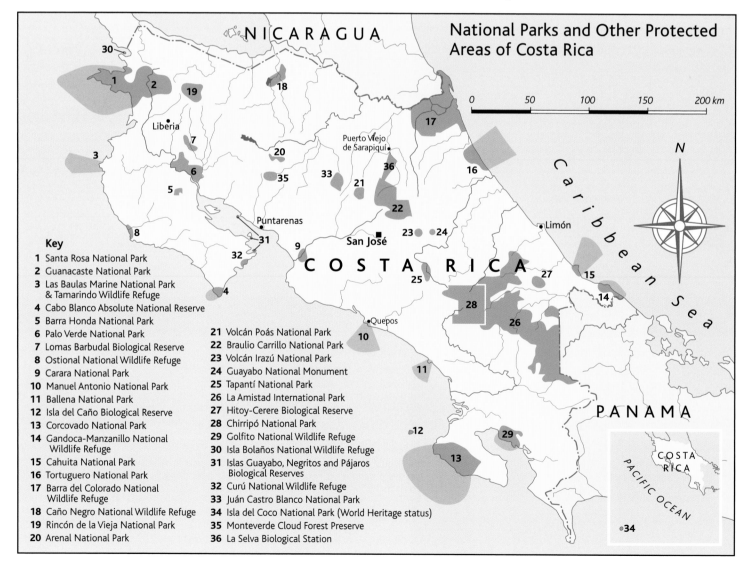

National Parks and Other Protected Areas of Costa Rica

Key
1 Santa Rosa National Park
2 Guanacaste National Park
3 Las Baulas Marine National Park & Tamarindo Wildlife Refuge
4 Cabo Blanco Absolute National Reserve
5 Barra Honda National Park
6 Palo Verde National Park
7 Lomas Barbudal Biological Reserve
8 Ostional National Wildlife Refuge
9 Carara National Park
10 Manuel Antonio National Park
11 Ballena National Park
12 Isla del Caño Biological Reserve
13 Corcovado National Park
14 Gandoca-Manzanillo National Wildlife Refuge
15 Cahuita National Park
16 Tortuguero National Park
17 Barra del Colorado National Wildlife Refuge
18 Caño Negro National Wildlife Refuge
19 Rincón de la Vieja National Park
20 Arenal National Park

21 Volcán Poás National Park
22 Braulio Carrillo National Park
23 Volcán Irazú National Park
24 Guayabo National Monument
25 Tapantí National Park
26 La Amistad International Park
27 Hitoy-Cerere Biological Reserve
28 Chirripó National Park
29 Golfito National Wildlife Refuge
30 Isla Bolaños National Wildlife Refuge
31 Islas Guayabo, Negritos and Pájaros Biological Reserves
32 Curú National Wildlife Refuge
33 Juán Castro Blanco National Park
34 Isla del Coco National Park (World Heritage status)
35 Monteverde Cloud Forest Preserve
36 La Selva Biological Station

was the site where Costa Ricans expelled the private army of the American William Walker in 1856.

In 1975, a large portion of rainforest on the Osa Peninsula was converted into Corcovado National Park in an attempt to protect the enormous biodiversity found there – it is estimated that up to half of the country's flora and fauna exist on this peninsula.

Tortuguero National Park on the north Caribbean coast was also created in 1975; a decision based strongly on the research findings of the Caribbean Conservation Corporation, which, directed by the zoologist and conservationist Archie Carr, had been studying the ecology of sea turtles around the village of Tortuguero for almost twenty years.

One of Costa Rica's largest national parks was created in 1977. In this year, a highway was constructed through the forested mountains of what is now Braulio Carrillo National Park. Fearing that the existence of this new road would trigger much more development in the area, conservation groups pressured the government into declaring the mountains surrounding the highway a national park.

The park is named Braulio Carrillo after Costa Rica's third ever president, who governed between 1837 and 1842 and was the first public figure to propose a land connection between the Central Valley and the Caribbean coast.

In 1982, the creation of La Amistad International Park in the south of Costa Rica placed an impressive 3,630 sq km of wilderness under the protection of the Costa Rican authorities. The park, which was designated a world heritage site by UNESCO in 1983, was a joint project with the government of Panama, where it encompasses a further 2,070 sq km of land. La Amistad is by far the largest national park in Costa Rica and borders no less than seven indigenous reserves on its Pacific and Caribbean slopes.

One of the most recently established national parks is that of Arenal, which wasn't designated a protected area until 1991. The boundaries of this park now protect over 120 sq km of wilderness, a large part of which is rainforest.

BELOW: *As well as its renowned turtle-nesting beach, Tortuguero National Park protects lowland rainforest and freshwater canals.*

ABOVE: *A strangler fig in Braulio Carrillo National Park – one of Costa Rica's largest protected wildernesses.*

THE FUTURE

The creation of the many protected wildernesses in Costa Rica has saved huge areas of tropical forest from destruction and provided habitats for a multitude of animal species that would have simply disappeared if the land had been cleared. However, urgent action is now required to maintain and inter-connect these areas in order to ensure the continued survival of the wildlife that lives within their boundaries. SINAC has been facing financial difficulties for several years and as a result it has not been able to provide the personnel, equipment and services that are required to maintain and protect its wild areas effectively. Even though it obtains a significant amount of income from the one million tourists that visit the parks each year, a large part of this money cannot be spent because of budget constraints placed upon it by other government depart-

ABOVE: *If the Jaguar (*Panthera onca*) is to survive, more biological corridors must be created to enlarge existing protected areas.*

ments. There is a lack of money available to pay the wages and equipment of park rangers and administrative personnel, and for education, training and employment that help to obtain the essential participation of local communities in the protection of the park or refuge they live next to.

In recent years, private donations from within Costa Rica and abroad have helped the situation enormously, though the decision by Costa Rican courts in 2007 to no longer permit government-employed park rangers to be paid directly by private foundations has put the parks in a perilous situation. For example, over 150 personnel from the Guanacaste and Osa Conservation Areas will lose their jobs if the government does not continue to finance their work.

In addition to maintenance and protection, national parks and other protected areas need to be interconnected to effectively increase their size. Almost all of the existing protected areas in Costa Rica are too small to sustain sizeable populations of large mammal such as the Jaguar, Spider Monkey and White-lipped Peccary, which require large areas of forest to provide them with enough food all year round. Also, small, isolated protected areas cause inbreeding within the mammalian species that are not able to leave these areas. As a consequence, fresh genetic material is not introduced into these species' populations, which eventually makes them more vulnerable to the spread of disease and genetic disorders.

Many birds also require large areas of forest in which to live. A lot of species migrate between different altitudes during the year in their search for seasonally available food. If a single protected area does not provide them with this range of altitudes, they have to travel between parks where the environment is much more hostile for them.

New forests that form biological corridors between existing protected areas are now essential if many of the animals that inhabit these areas are to survive in healthy and sustainable populations.

Dozens of biological corridor projects have been initiated in Costa Rica by both the government and private conservation organizations. A number have already achieved significant success, although they all require continued donations in order to purchase the land through which the corridors pass and rescue the protected areas of Costa Rica.

CHAPTER 6

CONSERVATION & ECOTOURISM

Like the other countries of the neotropics, Costa Rica has suffered the effects of deforestation, pollution, poaching and the illegal trade in wild animals. Despite the huge task at hand, however, the collective response to these threats has been significant; in addition to work carried out by the government, a healthy number of non-governmental and non-profit organizations are presently involved in conservation projects in Costa Rica.

LEFT: *The Jabiru (Jabiru mycteria) is an endangered stork that has benefited from conservation projects supported by the IUCN in Costa Rica.*

THE PROJECTS

A healthy number of non-profit and non-governmental organizations are involved in conservation projects in Costa Rica. The following is a selection of these. They all welcome publicity, donations or voluntary workers to continue realizing their aims.

Asociacion ANAI

www.anaicr.org

Since 1978, ANAI has been working with local people in the Talamanca mountains of the Caribbean slope to help them develop sustainable uses of the environment such as eco-tourism and ecologically friendly agricultural practices. ANAI have also helped to significantly reduce levels of poverty in the area. The organization was instrumental in the creation of the Gandoca-Manzanillo Wildlife Refuge and worked with the Nature Conservancy to establish the Talamanca-Caribbean Biological Corridor, which runs from the mountains of La Amistad National Park down to the ocean. ANAI also monitors and protects Leatherback Turtles on Gandoca Beach during the nesting season.

Association of Volunteers for Service in Protected Areas (ASVO)

www.asvocr.org

ASVO is an organization that is based in Costa Rica that arranges stays in the country's national parks for people wanting to do outdoor voluntary work.

Caribbean Conservation Corporation (CCC)

www.cccturtle.org

For almost fifty years the Florida-based CCC has been monitoring and protecting Green and Leatherback Turtles that nest in what is now Tortuguero National Park. They operate a data-gathering volunteer programme that has helped to understand more clearly the reproductive ecology of the two species. Their findings have demonstrated just how small and vulnerable the turtle populations are now, and this in turn has aided their conservation in Costa Rica.

Corcovado Foundation

www.corcovadofoundation.org

The work of this foundation has helped to provide a large number of new rangers and administrative personnel for protected areas in the Osa Peninsula in recent years. It has also obtained financial donations for essential equipment, training and the construction of a new park ranger station on the northern boundary of Corcovado National Park, called Los Planes. These advances have been crucial in the fight against illegal poachers in the area, who had decimated populations of animals such as the Jaguar and White-lipped Peccary. The Corcovado Foundation also runs an environmental education programme for local adults and children, and operates a turtle census project on the peninsula.

Friends of the Osa

www.osaconservation.org

The protection of the forests and coastal waters of the Osa Peninsula is the principal function of this organization. Friends of the Osa purchase land to guarantee its protection, and also help to manage and patrol wild areas in the region including the Osa National Wildlife Refuge and the Corcovado-Matapalo Biological Corridor. The organization also sells selected areas of land to conservation-minded buyers.

International Union for Conservation of Nature and Natural Resources (IUCN)

www.iucn.org

In Costa Rica, the IUCN has supported numerous conservation projects including the preservation of wetlands and river basins, the administration of protected areas and the scientific research required for these operations. The headquarters of IUCN maintains a 'red list' of threatened and endangered species from around the world, of which a significant number live in Costa Rica.

The Guanacaste Dry Forest Conservation Fund

www.rainmakerfoundation.org

The aim of this organization is to raise funds for the purchase of land that will increase the size of the Guanacaste Conservation Area. The new land includes a mountainous slope that will provide wildlife with a safe, forested corridor through which to travel during its seasonal migrations. The project is headed by the world-famous ecologist Professor Daniel H. Janzen, winner of the Crafoord Prize in Coevolutionary Ecology from the Swedish Royal Academy of Sciences and the Kyoto Prize in biological sciences from the Inamori Foundation.

OPPOSITE: *Green Turtles* (Chelonia mydas) *are both studied and protected in Costa Rica's Tortuguero National Park.*

The Leatherback Trust

www.leatherback.org

This trust is dedicated to the protection of Leatherback Turtles in Las Baulas Marine National Park in Guanacaste. It has educated park rangers and local residents about the threat these turtles face from poachers and some property developers, and demonstrated the financial gain the animals can bring to the community through well-regulated ecotourism. The Leatherback Trust played an important role in the establishment of the park in 1991.

The Nature Conservancy

www.nature.org

Many conservation projects in Costa Rica have received valuable support from the Nature Conservancy. Its guidance and financial donations have helped to maintain protected areas such as Corcovado National Park, as well as aiding the creation of biological corridors on the Osa Peninsula and in the mountains of Talamanca. Its help has also reached many local communities, assisting them to manage their resources appropriately and to earn an important income from ecotourism. The Nature Conservancy is also promoting the introduction of a water fee for private-sector industries, the proceeds of which would help finance the development of their local communities and the management of the surrounding natural resources.

The Organization for Tropical Studies (OTS)

www.ots.duke.edu

The OTS is a consortium of sixty-three universities and research centres from the United States, Australia and various countries in Latin America. It has three research stations surrounded by protected forest in Costa Rica that are open to visitors: La Selva in Sarapiquí, Las Cruces on the Pacific slope close to the Osa Peninsula and Palo Verde in Guanacaste. The organization is primarily concerned with research, although it is also involved in both local environmental education and the creation of two biological corridors between La Selva and Braulio Carrillo National Park, and between Las Cruces and the Guaymi Indigenous Reserve.

The Rainforest Alliance

www.rainforest-alliance.org

This organization provides sustainable tourism training for hotels and travel agencies in Costa Rica and other Latin American countries. It teaches participants how to operate their businesses in harmony with both nature and local populations and also help them to promote themselves within Costa Rica and abroad. On its website, the Alliance has a useful catalogue of businesses that it considers ecologically friendly, which can be found at www.eco-indextourism.org/en/home.

Tropical Science Centre (CCT)

www.cct.or.cr

The CCT (Centro Científico Tropical) has been dedicated to the research and conservation of natural resources in Costa Rica since 1962. It operates several small reserves and research stations, including the Monteverde Cloud Forest Preserve and Los Cusingos Neotropical Bird Sanctuary, which was the previous property of the late, renowned ornithologist Dr Alexander F. Skutch.

The marine conservation organization PROMAR, the Great Green Macaw Research and Conservation Project and the San Juan-La Selva Biological Corridor Project are also administered by members of the CCT.

World Wide Fund for Nature (WWF)

www.panda.org

The WWF has two valuable projects in Costa Rica. At Junquillal Beach in Guanacaste the organization works along with local villagers to protect nesting Leatherback Turtles and their hatchlings. WWF representatives have trained members of the local community to become nature guides, and have helped others to produce handicrafts that they can sell to tourists.

A second project is with fishermen on the Pacific coast. WWF members have helped to introduce the use of round fishing hooks that greatly reduce the number of sea turtles caught by long-line fishing methods. Fishermen have also received training that enables them to safely return turtles that are captured back into the sea.

Zoo Ave Wildlife Conservation Park and Education Centre

www.zooave.org

Zoo Ave has a wildlife education centre and wild animal rescue centre in La Garita de Alajuela. It receives over 1,000 decommissioned or injured wild animals a year – these are nursed and when possible, reintroduced into the wild in an appropriate habitat. Zoo Ave also has a breeding centre for endangered species such as the Scarlet Macaw, Green Macaw, Squirrel Monkey and Spider Monkey, and owns two private wildlife reserves where these animals are released into the wild.

TOP WILDLIFE-WATCHING LOCATIONS

Countless locations around Costa Rica offer great wildlife-watching opportunities in a whole range of different ecosystems. Some of them are within government-protected areas, others are in private reserves and a number are simply at the side of the road or viewable from a restaurant balcony. Below is a selection of some of the most exciting destinations where wildlife can be easily encountered.

LAS BAULAS MARINE NATIONAL PARK, GUANACASTE
Playa Grande, the main beach within this park, is one of just a few places in Costa Rica where the world's largest turtle, the Leatherback, comes ashore to nest. The female turtles emerge from the ocean at night and specially trained local guides accompany tourists along the beach in the darkness. Flash photography is not allowed, but torches with a red filter are used to subtly illuminate the rear end of the turtle as she lays

BELOW: *Playa Grande provides a great opportunity to see Leatherback Turtles (*Dermochelys coriacea*) nesting.*

her eggs in the sand. The memory of watching this process is worth much more than any photograph could be.

PALO VERDE NATIONAL PARK, GUANACASTE
The tropical dry forest that this park protects is a superb place to see many animals, especially mammals and birds. During the dry season, the lack of foliage makes animals much easier to spot and a watering hole can be a very rewarding place to sit and wait, where monkeys, deer, coatis, armadillos, peccaries and even the occasional cat arrive to quench their thirst. Palo Verde offers the unique opportunity to see two very differ-

ent ecosystems within the same park. A large, freshwater marsh sits in front of the park ranger station and the OTS station in the centre of the park, and during the first months of the year, thousands of waterbirds including spoonbills, storks, ibises, ducks and the Jabiru stork congregate in this lagoon to feed.

OSTIONAL WILDLIFE REFUGE, GUANACASTE

Once a month, between July and December, thousands of female Olive Ridley Turtles nest on the small beach at Ostional, Guanacaste, in an event known as an 'arribada'. Approximately six weeks after each arribada, the turtle hatchlings emerge from the sand and hurry down to the sea. Local villagers from this remote location of the Nicoya Peninsula act as guides for visitors who want to witness this magnificent natural spectacle.

THE RIVER TÁRCOLES, CENTRAL PACIFIC COAST

The main highway that weaves down to Jacó on the Pacific coast passes over the River Tárcoles at the northern boundary of Carara National Park. This bridge is an excellent viewpoint from which to see American Crocodiles as they bask on the sandbanks below. Sometimes more than ten individuals congregate along this section of the river, and a medium-sized telephoto lens is all that is needed to photograph them. As is the case with all wild animals, you should not try to throw food for them.

At dawn and dusk, Scarlet Macaws fly over the River Tárcoles on their journey to or from their feeding grounds in the forest of Carara National Park.

MANUEL ANTONIO NATIONAL PARK, CENTRAL PACIFIC COAST

The troops of White-faced Capuchins in Manuel Antonio have gained notoriety for their boldness towards tourists and also for the occasional theft of a packed lunch. However, these animals can be seen behaving quite naturally when they are not surrounded by humans, for example on the quieter trails or on weekdays during the low season.

The endangered Squirrel Monkey lives in and around this park, and Brown-throated Three-toed Sloths, Central American Agoutis and Black Spiny-tailed Iguanas are very common close to the beaches.

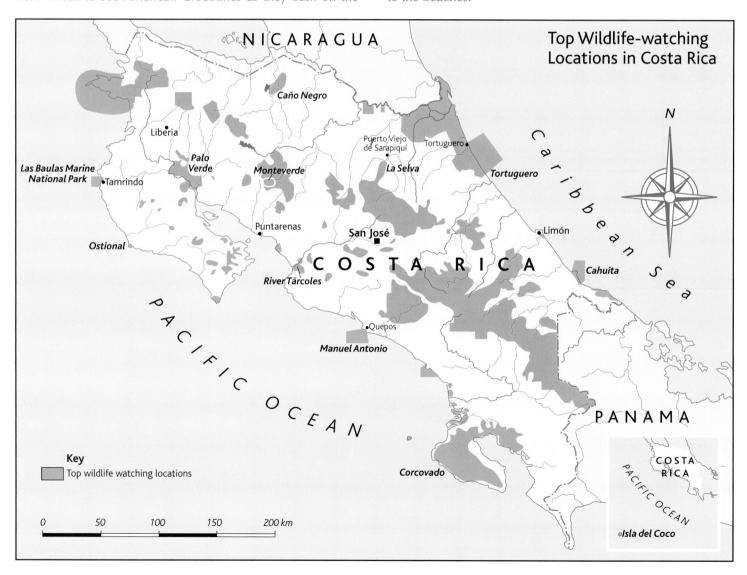

CORCOVADO NATIONAL PARK, OSA PENINSULA

Those visitors who are looking for adventure in Costa Rica are well rewarded by a trip to Corcovado National Park. The combination of gigantic rainforest trees and a lengthy, uninhabited coastline makes the area feel truly wild and remote. Scarlet Macaws, trogons, birds of prey, all four species of monkey, anteaters, crocodiles and Baird's Tapirs are commonly seen here, and knowing that Jaguars, Pumas and Ocelots prowl through the jungle adds an additional thrill to the experience.

A huge diversity of life exists around the Sirena Ranger Station in the centre of the park, which is reached by a day-long hike or a short flight in a small air taxi. Long walking trails enable visitors to thoroughly investigate the forest, beaches and rivers in the area, and one path continues for 20 km to the north-east, where it meets Los Patos Ranger Station on the park boundary.

RIGHT: *A White-faced Capuchin (*Cebus capucinus*) dozes briefly in Manuel Antonio National Park.*
BELOW: *The King Vulture (*Sarcoramphus papa*) is one of many rare animals that live in Corcovado National Park.*

ing the endangered Jabiru stork, the Anhinga and the Roseate Spoonbill. In addition, numerous caimans and crocodiles lurk in the water or sun themselves on the mud at the water's edge. The lagoon is usually reached by boat via the River Frío, which runs south from the small town of Los Chiles close to the Nicaraguan border. The rainforest that grows on the banks of this river is home to many more birds, monkeys and large lizards such as the Green Iguana and Emerald Basilisk. A slow boat cruise through these waters can be a very peaceful and rewarding experience for wildlife-watchers.

MONTEVERDE CLOUD FOREST PRESERVE, TILARÁN CORDILLERA

This privately owned preserve on the continental divide is one of the most famous forests in the neotropics. The main attraction is one of the most beautiful birds in the world, the Resplendent Quetzal, which nests here every year between March and June. Visitors to the preserve follow well-maintained trails through a misty forest draped with moss and epiphytes, passing under giant, prehistoric-looking palms and arcing bamboos. A team of very professional nature guides works at Monteverde; their knowledge and experience are invaluable in finding and identifying the many animals and plants that inhabit the forest. On a morning's guided walk, birds such as the quetzal, the Three-wattled Bellbird and the Black-faced Solitaire can be heard and possibly seen, and glasswing butterflies, orchids and a golden beetle may also be discovered.

ABOVE: *The epiphytic* Columea magnifica *in Monteverde Cloud Forest Preserve.*

CAÑO NEGRO WILDLIFE REFUGE, NORTHERN LOWLANDS

During the rainy season, a large lagoon forms on the plains of Caño Negro Wildlife Refuge. This becomes a feeding ground for thousands of migrant and non-migrant waterbirds, includ-

LA SELVA BIOLOGICAL STATION, SARAPIQUÍ

Few areas in Costa Rica boast as much biodiversity as the Caribbean rainforest at La Selva, situated on the northern boundary of Braulio Carrillo National Park. Within its 160 sq km of land, of which three-quarters are covered in primary rainforest, are 350 species of tree, over 100 species of mammal, 448 species of bird, more than 80 species of reptile (of which an astounding 50 are snakes) and many tens of thousands of invertebrates, including 500 species of ant. The reserve has 57 km of trails to explore, though a great deal of wildlife can be encountered during a relaxed, half-day stroll close to the station buildings. The number of tourists that visit the reserve is relatively low, so many more wild animals are seen in the forest than humans!

TORTUGUERO NATIONAL PARK, NORTH CARIBBEAN COAST

A network of freshwater canals meanders through the dense rainforest of Tortuguero National Park, and a boat trip along these natural waterways is a very different and exciting way of experiencing the jungle. Monkeys, sloths, basilisks, toucans, ospreys, kingfishers, and several species of heron are some of the most common animals that inhabit the trees overhanging the canals. Below them in the murky waters swim crocodiles, caimans, freshwater turtles, otters, 1.5 m-long Tropical Gar fish (*Atractosteus tropicus*) and the very rare West Indian Manatee.

Tortuguero National Park also includes a 35 km-long beach that is the nesting site of Green, Leatherback and Hawksbill Turtles. The Green Turtles arrive in the largest numbers between the months of June and November. Night turtle-watching tours operate in the park during this period, and as well as watching a female lay her eggs, visitors might see fresh Jaguar tracks in the sand.

CAHUITA NATIONAL PARK, SOUTH CARIBBEAN COAST

Cahuita is a great destination for those wanting a combination of exciting wildlife and some lazy hours on a quiet, tropical beach. A 7-km trail leads along the coastline from the sleepy village of Cahuita to the southern entrance of the park, called Puerto Vargas. On the

ABOVE: *Black River Turtles (*Rhinoclemmys funerea*) bask on a floating log in Tortuguero National Park.*
BELOW: *A leaf-cutter ant carries a leaf fragment back to its nest in Cahuita National Park.*

way, it crosses small creeks and rivers where Boat-billed Herons, Green Ibises, enormous blue land crabs and Spectacled Caimans feed in the shadows. Animals that are common around the Puerto Vargas Ranger Station include Mantled Howler Monkeys, two-toed and three-toed sloths, leaf-cutter ants and Eyelash Vipers.

WILDLIFE GUIDES & REFERENCE VOLUMES

Dressler, Robert L., *Field Guide to the Orchids of Costa Rica and Panama*, Cornell University Press, 1993

Fogden, Michael and Patricia, *Hummingbirds of Costa Rica*, Zona Tropical Publications, Costa Rica, 2005

Garrigues, Richard and Robert Dean, *The Birds of Costa Rica: A Field Guide*, Cornell University Press/Zona Tropical Publications, 2007

Janzen, Daniel H., *Costa Rican Natural History*, University of Chicago, 1993

Leenders, Twan, *A Guide to Amphibians and Reptiles of Costa Rica*, Zona Tropical Publications, Costa Rica, 2001

Murillo Aguilar, Katiana, *Costa Rica Volcanoes*, Fundación Neotropica, Costa Rica, 2003

Styles, Gary L. and Skutch, Alexander F., *A Guide to the Birds of Costa Rica*, Cornell University Press, 1989

Wainwright, Mark, *The Natural History of Costa Rican Mammals*, Zona Tropical Publications, Costa Rica, 2002

Zuchowski, Willow, *A Guide to Tropical Plants of Costa Rica*, Zona Tropical Publications, Costa Rica, 2005

USEFUL CONTACTS

Costa Rica Wildlife and Landscape Photography Tours
with Adrian Hepworth
www.hepworthimages.com

Custom-made tours in Costa Rica
www.centralamerica.com

The Costa Rican Tourist Board
www.visitcostarica.com

The Rainforest Alliance
Planning Ecotourism Holidays in Costa Rica
www.eco-indextourism.org/en/home

National System of Conservation Areas of Costa Rica
www.sinaccr.net

Costa Rican Ministry of the Environment and Energy
www.minae.go.cr

National Meteorological Institute of Costa Rica
www.imn.ac.cr

INDEX

PICTURE CREDITS

Principle Photography All photographs by Adrian Hepworth/NHPA/Photoshot, unless otherwise specified below.

For more information on Adrian's work, visit www.hepworthimages.com or contact Adrian at adrian@hepworthimages.com

Additional Photography Mark Bowler/NHPA/Photoshot, 131 (bottom); James Carmichael, Jr./NHPA/Photoshot, 84, 97; Bill Coster/NHPA/ Photoshot, 86, 162; Stephen Dalton/NHPA/ Photoshot, 122 (left); Stephen Krasemann/NHPA/Photoshot, 132; B. Jones & M. Shimlock/NHPA/Photoshot, 68; Harold Palo, Jr./NHPA/ Photoshot, 122; Otto Pfister/NHPA/Photoshot, 169 (right); Jany Sauvanet/NHPA/Photoshot, 100 (bottom), 130, 133 (bottom); Kevin Schafer/NHPA/Photoshot, 83; Tom & Therisa Stack/NHPA/Photoshot, 131 (top); Monica Ulett, back jacket flap.

ACKNOWLEDGEMENTS

This project could not have been completed had it not been for the constant support of my beloved wife Cindy. *Wild Costa Rica* is dedicated to her and our dear sons, Pablo and Benjamin.

I am extremely grateful to the following people who have helped directly in the production of *Wild Costa Rica*: my editors Krystyna Mayer and Simon Papps at New Holland Publishers in London, Tim Harris and Lee Dalton from the Natural History Photo Agency (NHPA), Patricia Alpízar at Costa Rica's Ministry of the Environment and Energy (MINAE), Professor Daniel H. Janzen of the Rainmaker Foundation, Mariana Mora at the Organization for Tropical Studies (OTS) in San José and Dr Eugenio Gonzalez J, the Director of the OTS Biological Station in Palo Verde,

Randal García, the Director of Conservation at INBio, Dulce Wilson of the Friends of Monteverde Cloud Forest, Robert Sequiera at the Caño Negro Wildlife Refuge, Sylvia Chaves from IUCN Costa Rica and the authors Willow Zuchowski and Twan Leenders.

I also owe my thanks to the numerous park rangers, naturalist guides and researchers who have enriched my knowledge of Costa Rica and its wildlife over the last fifteen years.

The family and friends who have always encouraged and helped my work in Costa Rica receive my sincere gratitude as always. In particular, a special, heartfelt thank you goes to Mum and Dad, Pete, Jan, Iona, Sarah, Jamie, Chloe, Andy, Matt, Victor, Maria, Norman, Margarita and Mónica.